Coaching Essentials

2nd edition

Coaching Essentials

2nd edition

Practical, proven techniques for world-class executive coaching

Patricia Bossons Ph.D, Jeremy Kourdi
and Denis Sartain

B L O O M S B U R Y

LONDON • NEW DELHI • NEW YORK • SYDNEY

First published in United Kingdom in 2012 by

Bloomsbury Publishing Plc
50 Bedford Square
London
WC1B 3DP
www.bloomsbury.com

A CIP record for this book is available from the British Library.

ISBN: 9-781-4081-5720-6

This book is produced using paper that is made from wood grown in managed, sustainable forests. It is natural, renewable and recyclable. The logging and manufacturing processes conform to the environmental regulations of the country of origin.

Design by Fiona Pike, Pike Design, Winchester
Typeset by Saxon Graphics, Derby
Printed in the United Kingdom by Clays

CONTENTS

PREFACE TO THE SECOND EDITION

Since the first edition of *Coaching Essentials* was published in 2009, we have seen the development of a range of new themes in coaching which have become widely adopted and part of many coaches' practice. Our intention in this new edition is to highlight some of the most popular themes and to help readers become more aware of how to incorporate them into their own coaching.

As with all the tools, techniques and insights in *Coaching Essentials*, we aim to bring to your attention areas of coaching which might be useful and helpful, and to then give you the information you need to be able to follow up in more detail those which appeal. We also link each of the new topics to the tools and techniques in the rest of the book, as well as suggesting a few new ones.

As coaching develops and moves towards increasing levels of professionalism, many different models of practice and application come to our attention. As we develop as coaches ourselves, it is important to keep abreast of new thinking and developments while, at the same time, always keeping a core sense of who we are as coaches. It is always our personal stance and style which makes us the coach we are. New understanding, tools, techniques and models are all extremely valuable, equally important is how we incorporate them into our individual approach to coaching. These themes of continuing development and self-awareness are probably the most important of all. 'Coaching supervision' is the one topic which we would encourage everyone engaging with coaching – whether formally or informally – to build into their practice.

Some general themes we are noticing at the moment include:

■ **organisations are adopting coaching as a core management approach, and bringing coaching for individuals in-house. At the very top of organisations, the executive level, external coaches are still being used. As the use of coaching cascades down to other levels in organisations, there is an increasing requirement for coaching skills to be part of a manager's repertoire, in order to meet demand. This then opens up a whole new range of challenges** around the boundaries between line management and coaching. Again, the provision of coaching supervision within organisations is an essential way to support managers working their way through this minefield.

- **Team coaching,** often using an external coach. This is becoming better understood and more widely used.
- **The re-emergence of mentoring** as a formal intervention within organisations. The development of coaching skills for mentors is another area of development.
- **More formal research is being done in the field of coaching.** In particular, there are a number of large-scale studies being carried out to try and gain more understanding of what makes for an effective coaching relationship, with the emphasis on the relationship.

The new themes we have chosen to develop further in this book are in Part 4. Before then, as in the first edition, we look at the commonly presented, and more difficult, challenges coaches can be faced with. We have collected these issues from our experience of working with over 800 coaches and managers involved in our coaching skills development programmes, so our information and insights are very much practitioner-based.

We hope you find the new edition stimulating and useful – you may want to take ideas from it and develop them much further for yourself, or you may just want to dip into it during your everyday coaching. Either way, we wish you every success in your vital, valuable work as a coach.

PART ONE

SUCCEEDING AS A COACH

CHAPTER 1

THE CASE FOR COACHING

The popularity and impact of coaching continues to develop and grow all over the world. It is, perhaps, entirely appropriate that an activity that helps individuals to develop their skills, achieve their potential and succeed is itself developing, achieving and succeeding. Despite its perennial popularity and success, however, there's no room for complacency. The early years of the 21st century continue to be a time of accelerating change, with major opportunities (resulting, for example, from technology and globalisation) as well as significant, sudden pressures on leaders in general and businesses in particular. In these circumstances, it's worth asking: *why work with a coach?*

First, we should explain that our area of expertise is coaching people within organisations. In this role, we've worked with hundreds of individuals not only as coaches, but also as teachers, helping others to develop their own coaching skills. Our case for coaching, presented in this book, is based on our personal experience and practical observations. These are based largely on observing people who are actually coaching, but our thinking is also influenced by those who employ coaches on behalf of their organisations.

In our experience, coaching enables individuals to step back from their day-to-day pressures, with the dedicated support of a skilled professional. This can help individuals (whom we refer to as *clients* or *coachees*) focus on resolving the challenges they face and, ultimately, enhance their performance and that of their organisation. Individuals who've worked with an executive coach typically report that doing so played a valuable role in enabling them to achieve their business and personal objectives.

We find that a quantitative, bottom-line justification of the return on investment for executive coaching is a challenge frequently posed to the providers of such services. The real answer always has to be the somewhat frustrating 'It depends...'. However, studies such as those by Malcolm Higgs and Victor Dulewicz at Henley Business School show that the most statistically significant factors contributing to the successful career progression of individuals, following their MBA studies, were neither attributable to factors of traditional intelligence (IQ) nor factors of management competency frameworks (MQ) but to factors of emotional intelligence (EQ).

Also, within the range of emotional intelligence, Higgs and Dulewicz found that the most statistically significant factors contributing to career success (as measured by increases in job position and salary) were *self-awareness* and *emotional resilience*. We would certainly argue that the best way to help people to develop their self-awareness and emotional resilience (two longstanding and widely recognised attributes of great leaders) would be to include coaching alongside other development activities, such as 360-degree feedback and experiential development.

The coaching relationship is unique in comparison with the variety of other relationships we might have in our lives. It's probably the only non-therapeutic relationship where we can have a conversation with another person with the attention solely upon us – the coachees. It's not reciprocal: we don't have to listen to their issues in return for them listening to us. Perhaps most importantly, we don't have to worry about taking care of the personal relationship as well as having the conversation. We don't need to edit how we say something or the content of what we say to preserve any relationship other than the one of coach-coachee.

A good coaching conversation is non-directive, non-judgemental and full of what the influential American psychologist Carl Rogers would have called 'unconditional positive regard' (see, for example, his books *On Becoming a Person*, *Client-Centered Therapy* and *Freedom to Learn*). This is something that we generally have far too little of and upon which everyone's psychological well-being often depends.

Recent research by Diane Coutu and Carol Kauffman (see *What Can Coaches Do For You?* published in the *Harvard Business Review*, January 2009) surveyed 140 leading coaches, with five experts commenting on the findings. This work shows the lack of unanimity about coaching, with the article highlighting that: 'The coaching field is filled with contradictions. Coaches themselves disagree over why they're hired, what they do and how to measure success'.

It seems to us that, while coaching continues to produce great results for individuals and organisations, the reasons why companies engage coaches have altered. In the past, most companies engaged a coach to deal with destructive behaviour at senior levels. Today, most coaching is undertaken to help develop the capabilities of high-potential performers.

For example, Coutu and Kauffman found that three quarters of the people who buy coaching do so for three reasons: to develop high-potential executives, to facilitate a transition to a new role or to act as a sounding board. Only 12 per cent of respondents use coaching to address derailing behaviour. This view is supported by our own experience. We've certainly seen this shift from coaching being viewed as a remedial activity, when performance is suffering, to an aspirational activity. Simply put, executives know their company values them if they're provided with a coach.

The research highlights several other interesting aspects about the current state of executive coaching. For example, 29 per cent of research respondents view professional certification as 'very necessary' – a view that we would certainly support. In such a popular, significant, influential and potentially lucrative area of activity as executive coaching, it's vital that minimum standards are maintained and some level of formal quality control is exercised. The issue is one of professionalism and quality: executive coaches need formal certification and companies buying coaching should demand it. Furthermore, the issue of certification dovetails with the need for coaches to be professionally supervised.

Research also reveals that coaching assignments are typically between seven and 12 months in duration, and the median hourly cost of coaching is US$500. Finally, while only 3 per cent of coaches are hired to address personal issues, 76 per cent of coaches report assisting executives with personal matters. Again, this is a revealing point: coaching requires that, as professionals, we relate to the whole individual. The skills, issues and behaviours that coaches seek to address or enhance with their clients are influenced by numerous factors, over a long period. In fact, 76 per cent seems a surprisingly low figure.

So, for us and the clients we work with, the benefits are clear. One-to-one coaching complements other types of leadership development and helps individuals:

- **lead people as productively as possible;**
- **devise a programme of self-development based on day-to-day issues;**
- **create a plan or strategy for improving skills;**

- prepare and implement plans for their personal, professional and career development;
- review progress to ensure that the maximum learning is taken from each situation or experience.

Executives work in pressurised environments where time is precious. A personalised development programme geared to an individual's own agenda, pace and timescale is one of the key advantages. Using an experienced executive coach, especially one who has a personal understanding of how business and commerce operate at the highest levels, can be a highly effective means of learning and benefiting the bottom line.

Area of focus	Personal benefits for the executive	People-related (HR) benefits	Business benefits
Resolving problems and achieving major changes within the business	• Maintain the executive's focus, providing support and preventing 'burnout'. • Ensure that executives in new situations are aligned with issues such as culture, responsibilities and operating styles – and quickly achieve success. • Reduce stress and emotional factors that interfere with performance.	• Retain, develop and attract the most talented, experienced and valuable employees. • Reduce rivalry and conflict that obstructs collaboration among executive team members. • Close the gap in leadership skills between leaders' current expertise and what is required of them.	• Provide timely support for individuals who'll lead new initiatives and implement strategies. • Remove behavioural obstacles that interfere with implementing strategic initiatives and goals. • Eliminate obstacles encountered by executives who are assuming new roles.
Developing skills and effectiveness	• Increase the level of skills and knowledge – especially valuable in complex or rapidly changing businesses. • Improve the executive's work–life balance. • Improve the use of emotional intelligence.	• Develop management and leadership skills among 'technical' people. • Ensure the success of leaders in the early stages of their new leadership position. • Develop the capacity to provide feedback and develop the right behaviours, culture and approach.	• Co-ordinate – and ensure involvement in – succession planning. • Maximise the development of high-potential employees. • Improve strategic thinking and leadership capabilities.

ABOUT THIS BOOK

In the pages that follow, we're aiming simply to share our practical experiences of working with many people involved in the executive coaching world. This refers mainly to the three main 'stakeholders' in the business coaching relationship: the *coach*, the *coachee* (or client) and the *organisation* (or employer) – that is, those who are commissioning, sanctioning and paying for the coaching.

The tools, techniques and applications of coaching we consider here aren't given as prescriptive advice. Indeed, we hope that we've presented it very much in a coaching frame, offering knowledge and information, getting you to think about your own specific circumstances, and giving you the support you need while you come up with your own solutions.

The book is divided into five parts.

- **Part 1 explains how to succeed as a coach. As well as setting out the case for coaching, we highlight (in the next chapter) the essential skills that coaches need.**
- **Part 2 is concerned with difficult challenges for coaches: what they are, the issues to consider and possible solutions. These challenges can be particularly daunting or problematic and while some are commonplace others are, thankfully, quite rare.**
- **Part 3 addresses some of the typical challenges that coaches encounter. A few may seem complex while others are quite simple, but they are all important, and adopting the right approach when handling these issues is essential. As well as explaining these issues, this section also provides possible questions for coaches in each circumstance, as well as suggesting techniques that might help.**
- **Part 4 gives an overview of some of the emerging themes in executive coaching at the time this second edition went to press. A brief summary of each area is given with suggestions for further follow up if desired.**
- **Part 5 provides a varied range of proven coaching tools and techniques. Some, such as the Myers-Briggs type indicator, are firmly established favourites, while others may be a little less well**

known. All of these techniques, however, are proven and have achieved results. Each idea is briefly summarised, with guidance provided about the type of technique and when to use it. Most useful and important, however, is a practical guide to applying each technique and ensuring success.

■ Part 6 comprises a bibliography and suggested further reading.

We've collaborated to provide practical guidance and support to anyone who's involved in the exciting, challenging and rewarding world of executive coaching. We hope that the ideas and questions we suggest and the experiences we share will help you to develop and prosper as a coach.

CHAPTER 2

ESSENTIAL SKILLS FOR COACHES

What are the most important skills for a coach? Well, careful, intelligent questioning is clearly vital but other skills are also essential. This chapter highlights the most important skills that executive coaches need to possess and develop.

UNDERSTANDING WHAT COACHES DO – AND WHAT THEY AVOID

What coaches do	Why it's a strength...	...and how it can become a weakness
Take control and be given control (coachees are in your hands and give you authority as their coach).	• Provides clarity, focus, reassurance. • Challenges and provokes. • Is directive. • Gets through to people.	• Undermines the coach's own thought processes and may become disempowering. • Misses some issues in the need for control – e.g. it may mean the coach fails to focus on patient, sensitive exploration of issues.
Question	• Shows interest, provides a feeling of support and builds rapport. • Uncovers, explores and builds on issues, goals, options, realities, ideas and potential changes. • Allows coachees to think about issues in a different way.	• Can become tiresome or fatuous, with diminishing value or returns – like a child constantly asking 'why?' • Can become uncomfortable – so *how, when* and *why* the question is asked invariably matters as much as the question itself.
Discuss issues	Reframing provides a valuable new perspective. Simply saying or hearing an issue described can provide a new perspective.	Too much talking can stunt conversation, distract, miss key issues and lead to coachees feeling disempowered. The balance of talking should usually be in favour of the coachees – it's their session!
Challenge basic assumptions	Encourages coachees to find ideas and a way forward by: • removing constraints; • highlighting new opportunities; • providing a different way of thinking and a different reality to the one originally perceived.	There are so many assumptions that it's vital to find the most relevant ones to challenge. If not, it may distract, irritate or simply be irrelevant.

What coaches do	Why it's a strength...	...and how it can become a weakness
Use models and techniques	• Provides energy, focus and a new perspective. • Offers guidance. • Stimulates thinking into new areas. • Can de-personalise an issue and make it easier to consider.	• Models must be relevant and given in the right way at the right time, or they will be ineffective. • Can be simple but not trivial – they need to be relevant, valuable and practical. • Can result in a reliance on techniques. • Can get in the way and break rapport. • May seem 'clunky', disrupting the flow or intensity of a conversation.
Summarise, reframe, set goals for the future and keep in touch with these goals	• Keeps the conversation 'on track' and ensures that progress is achieved. • Maintains and builds momentum during the conversation. • Presses home the key points and ensures these are not lost, forgotten or dismissed.	• The coach or coachee can become fixated on a goal and rush towards a plan – missing some important issues along the way. • The coach can forget to check in at times to see if the goal has changed.

ESTABLISHING YOUR INTENT

It's important and useful to establish your *intent as a coach* at various stages of the coaching process. This includes before and during your training as a coach, after you qualify, before you seek business, before your first coaching session and when you talk or introduce yourself to a coachee. To establish your intent, ask yourself the questions below.

- **Why am I doing this? What is my intent?**
- **When I accept a brief, what is my intent?**
- **When I work with coachees, what is my intent for them? Have I explained this clearly to them?**

If you aren't clear about your own intent, how can you expect any one else to be?

LISTENING AND EMPATHY

There are several simple steps that can help coaches to improve their listening and empathy skills. These are essential if the coaches are to succeed.

- Focus on what people are *really* saying, not on what you *think* they're saying.
- Put yourself in the other person's position.
- 'Speak their language' – get your message across in terms that others will respond to and understand.
- Use questioning and reflection as ways of improving understanding, testing assumptions and showing that you're listening.
- Summarise key points in the conversation, thus preventing misunderstandings and moving the conversation on to the next point.
- Maintain professionalism and control emotions.
    - Be critically aware and react to ideas, not people.
    - Focus on the significance to the discussion of the facts and evidence.
    - Avoid jumping to conclusions.
    - Listen for how things are said, and what is not said.
- Avoid making quick decisions – instead, give yourself time to think and react.
- Remember to recognise your own views and biases.
- Don't ignore body language – yours and theirs.
- Be sensitive and tactful, especially when disagreeing or questioning. Choose your words carefully, outlining your views.

TECHNIQUES FOR IMPROVING LISTENING SKILLS

- Keep a notebook and routinely record key points either during discussions and meetings, if coachees are comfortable with this, or immediately afterwards. This is a journalistic skill; as well as providing a valuable record for future reference, it'll also train you to listen actively.

■ Develop your knowledge, understanding and use of body language. Understanding non-verbal communication is a valuable way to uncover how people feel as well as what they think about an issue.

■ Prepare to empathise by considering how you might react or behave in the specific situation. Consider what motivations would drive possible reactions. Find out about different causes of motivation, the beliefs and values held by the coachee.

■ Seek specific feedback. The more specific the feedback you obtain, the easier it'll be for you to track progress and develop this skill.

PLANNING FOR THE FIRST SESSION

How do you prepare for the first session with a new client? Several steps are especially useful. First, get acquainted with, as far as possible, the organisation's situation and any useful background information. It's also valuable to:

■ prepare to establish overall goals through questioning and feedback;

■ explore the current situation and establish expectations;

■ plan a selection of strategies to achieve goals, including how you and the client will work together;

■ evaluate and select the best approach;

■ agree on the next steps and create an action plan.

Subsequent sessions should include feedback and evaluation of previous sessions, goals and plans. Also, subsequent goals should be set to establish an agenda for the next session.

BEING PATIENT

It can take coachees time to feel comfortable with their coach. This may only be a few minutes but it cannot be rushed. Instead, what matters is the quality of questioning, meaning the relevance, impact and ability to provoke ideas or reveal truths. Getting a coachee to 'open up' relies on:

■ **patient, persistent and respectful questioning;**
■ **sufficient trust and respect;**
■ **time – sufficient time for trust and respect to be established, bearing in mind that this might take different amounts of time for different people.**

COACHING ROLES AND RESPONSIBILITIES

Who's involved	Their role	Responsibilities
Executive coaches • Experienced, credible individuals. • Possess a comprehensive understanding of organisational, leadership and interpersonal issues. • Self-aware and able to recognise and manage their own responses and emotions. • Understand the basic dimensions of human needs and thinking processes.	• Helping to identify and define a clear coaching agenda – with the executives. • Listening carefully to the executives and helping them to analyse their situation systematically. • Encouraging the executives to be honest and realistic about their goals and ambitions. • Helping the executives to assess their abilities, potential and aspirations accurately. • Exploring the executives' assumptions, behaviours and values – and challenging their effectiveness. • Facilitating the coaching process so that the executives identify their own solutions to the challenges they face. • Encouraging the executives to improve the way they work.	• Creating a safe, supportive environment for the coaching. • Keeping confidential all material discussed with the executives (unless disclosed with their permission). • Maintaining appropriate boundaries between themselves and the executives – ensuring the executives don't become dependent on their coach. • Keeping the programme supervisor informed of the progress of the coaching programme (though not the content) in line with the agreed coaching contract. • Ensuring that, as coaches, they have appropriate supervision arrangements for themselves. • Ensuring that each coach, coachee and the organisation have agreed expectations of coaching and uphold this contract.

Who's involved	Their role	Responsibilities
Executives (the coachees) Invariably senior executives in the organisation or those whose impact is significant (and will therefore derive greatest benefit for the business by being coached).	• Learning to understand the issues and challenges they face by working with the coaches. • Identifying ways to address their challenges. • Taking action in the workplace as a result of their coaching. • Developing themselves as a result of their coaching.	• Being open and honest with the coaches. • Gaining the maximum benefit from the coaching programme (keeping appointments, focusing on the issues raised and remaining with the programme). • Implementing actions that emerge as a result of the coaching programme.

Programme supervisors Usually individuals from within the training and development department. They should be senior individuals, not directly connected to the executives, who possess an understanding of the process of executive coaching.	• Facilitating implementation of the coaching relationship:
	  ○ working with the executives and their line managers to understand the priorities and goals;
	  ○ finding appropriate executive coaches.
	• Acting as a 'bridge', when appropriate, between the coaches and line managers, to ensure the coaching remains aligned with the business's needs.
	• Reviewing the process with the executives to ensure their needs are being addressed.
	• Ensuring appropriate evaluation of the coaching.
		• Respecting issues of confidentiality and the coaching boundaries.
		• Representing the organisation's part in the coaching contract.

Line managers (or sponsoring executives) The executives' line managers should help to establish the goals of the programme. They should remain close to the process and help the executives implement any changes.	• Discussing their expectations with the coaches and programme supervisors. • Providing feedback on the executives' performance before, during and after the programme.	• Allowing the executives time to prepare and participate. • Agreeing funding. • Helping to create a working environment that supports the executives, enabling them to implement the changes they want.

Who's involved	Their role	Responsibilities
HR professionals (or HR business partners) They will have an understanding of development, people management and business issues and are likely to have a close working relationship with the executives and their line managers.	• Often involved in the initial phase of the process by: ○ helping to analyse the issues the executives are seeking to address; ○ determining whether executive coaching is the most appropriate solution.	Helping to ensure that the working environment can support the changes the executives may be seeking to introduce.

RECOGNISING THAT PERSONAL ISSUES ARE SIGNIFICANT

In the majority of cases, personal issues play an important part in the highly varied areas being discussed. Of course, this may not always necessarily be the case, but if personal issues are interpreted broadly to include the perceptions arising from coachees' experiences, the way they think and the reasons for thinking that way, then such issues will invariably be significant. Most coaching issues are personal. If they were purely task-related, then a manager or consultant would be used.

This has an important implication for coaches: they should recognise that personal issues may be a factor, and without prejudging the issue be prepared to ask, understand and empathise. Or, viewed another way, don't be surprised or thrown off balance if personal issues suddenly arise. In this situation empathy and understanding are vital and the key at these moments of revelation, which at times might even be emotional, is to remain focused on the issue in hand, or be prepared to move to another issue if this seems to be what the coachee would prefer.

Invariably, 'personal' issues will arise. People act as whole beings and, mostly, don't divide their thoughts, values or beliefs into separate compartments.

FOLLOWING A CLEAR PROCESS

There are several other valuable points to remember when coaching.

- **Set clear goals** for the discussion and then keep in touch with these throughout the conversation – if only in your mind. These goals may take time to emerge, but once they're agreed ensure that the conversation achieves or progresses these goals – or else agree to re-evaluate and establish new ones.
- **Recognise that goals may be overtaken by other issues.** If that's the case, then be explicit about what is happening, agree new goals in the new area, and move on.
- **Don't overlook process issues** in the rush to establish rapport or support the coachees. Process issues (e.g. timing, follow-up arrangements) are essential.
- **Summarise and review progress regularly.** This is valuable for reflecting, sustaining a line of questioning or exploration, and clarifying the coachees' thinking as well as the coaches'. It also helps keep the conversation from meandering off the point or away from the agreed goals.
- **Avoid making assumptions** – both explicit and implicit. This is a vital challenge and can, perhaps, be accomplished by asking questions that are simple – even obvious – relevant and insightful. Also, this is a useful way to press and probe, and may reveal even more information. Coaches need to check their own assumptions, as well as challenging those of their coachees.
- **Get the right balance between listening, questioning and introducing new ideas and concepts.** This is essential for the session to be fully effective without losing pace, focus or rapport.
- **Provide relevant ideas and concepts** in an interesting, stimulating way to get coachees thinking about the issues.

CONFIDENTIALITY

The confidentiality of the discussions between the executives and their coaches is fundamental to the integrity of the process. The coaches should only disclose the coaching content with express permission. However, the coaches will normally provide information about progress to key stakeholders, who may include the line managers. The nature of this process will be agreed with the stakeholders at the beginning of the coaching contract.

COACHING FOR BEHAVIOURAL CHANGE

'Two human beings sit facing one another. One is called a therapist and the other, a client. This second person, the client, is unhappy, dissatisfied with his present life; feels stuck, blocked; experiences pain in his life. The therapist is faced with the task of assisting the client to change in a way which will allow him to grow, allow him more choices, more satisfaction, and less pain in his life. What, exactly, is the task that the therapist, this people-helper, will accomplish when he assists the client in changing?'[1]

The Structure of Magic

Our understanding of the task of a people-helper is:

All therapists are confronted with the problem of responding adequately to such people. Responding adequately in this context means to us assisting in changing the clients' experience in some way which enriches it. Rarely do therapists accomplish this by changing the world. Their approach then is typically to change the clients' experience of the world. People do not operate directly on the world, but operate necessarily on the world through their perception or model of the world. Therapists, then, characteristically operate to change the client's model of the world and consequently, the client's behaviour and experience....

This quote, from the originators of NLP, is directly referring to the world of therapy. However, if you read it again and substitute the word 'coach' for 'therapist', you might feel, as we do, that it is a very useful way of thinking about the coaching process as well.

As we point out throughout this book, coaches do not bring with them the answers to life's problems and dilemmas, and even if they believe they have the answers to the issues that clients present to them for discussion, that is not the nature of the contract. We have referred to boundaries and boundary management that deal specifically with what coachees can expect from coaches and what coaches are able to offer coachees. Context

---

1   Bandler, Richard and John Grinder. *The Structure of Magic*. Science & Behaviour Books, 1976.

is key here: these offerings and expectations will take place either in organisational or private environments, but they are ultimately governed by the degree to which coaches feel bound by ethical considerations.

That said, the paragraphs above illustrate the true nature of coaching. As coaches, people-helpers, we sit opposite people who bring with them their experiences of the world. The way in which they behave or act within it is the direct result of the way in which they have made sense of the world via their cognitive processes, experiences, cultures and neuroses. While we may share similar experiences, the way in which we view them may not be the same; in fact, they may be totally different because of all these processes. We share, introduce and discuss the possibilities, limitations and similarities that all this information from others gives us and from this discussion, coachees are often able to produce behavioural change or even maintain equilibrium.

Any credible coaching training will assiduously spend time teaching potential coaches about the nature of personal reality, the subjective experience and how behaviour is governed by the way we think about the way we are or the way the world is, as well as our personal 'truths'. Our truths are often generalisations we have made about a single event, person or the world at large. Some of the strongest opinions often lack substance or have little evidence to uphold them yet still have enormous impact: many significant events – good and bad – in personal lives as well as on the national or international stage have occurred as the result of unsubstantiated or misguided beliefs.

But in coaching, for instance, so much of what a person can achieve is governed by what they believe about themselves, and what a person believes about themselves may not be the same as what others believe about them. So who *should* they believe?

Very often, we are limited by our doubts about our ability to achieve rather than our ability itself. Many coaches have been described as 'inspirational' because they have been able to question successfully their coachees' lack of belief, challenging them to believe something different, and that same person has then gone on to achieve what they once thought was beyond them.

'If you think you can do a thing or think you can't do a thing, you're right.'
Henry Ford, US automobile industrialist (1863–1947)

Challenging a limiting belief can be done through questioning to find out details around it such as:

■ **according to whom is this true?**
■ **when did you believe this to be true?**
■ **what did you believe about the subject *before* you found this out (establishing a time when the limiting belief was not held)?**

Nancy Kline elegantly challenges beliefs when she asks, 'What are you most assuming that is stopping you from going forward? Do you think that assumption is true? What is true and liberating instead? If you knew that... how would you move forward?'[2]

All of these questions do not seek to give the holder of beliefs another one to replace it, but rather to establish the process through which they came to hold that belief. In other words, in seeking to find out *how* something comes about, we can throw a light on what might be a flawed *process*. This emphasis on process runs through so many models and techniques used as enablers in coaching.

Coaching draws on the techniques, concepts and principles of Psychotherapy, Cognitive Behavioural Therapy, Gestalt Therapy, Person Centred Counselling, Hypnosis, Linguistics, systems thinking and Behaviourism and uses them to enable people to understand how present choices and outcomes are affected by how we choose to think. All of these disciplines have one thing in common: they are involved in the study of human behaviour.

Coaches often find that coachees do not know they have a choice about *how* they think – they just think. In fact, it is a revelation to many people that we have any choice at all about what and who we choose to believe. They accept their reality as the only reality and so continue to live in it, good or bad.

How we behave and the results we achieve in our lives not only depend on how we think (which in turn affects how we act), but also how we think in different contexts and within different groups, within different

---

2 Kline, Nancy. *More Time to Think*. Fisher King Publishing, 2009.

environments. We can be affected within organisations by the group that we become part of or are assigned to. Once we are part of a group, we take on a role outside of the tasks we are given. Belbin's team roles is a classic model that describes how we can produce a behaviour that we stick to within a team. This in turn produces expectations from other team or group members that lock us into that behaviour, sometimes regardless of choice because it has become an expectation of the group. This group dynamic is a powerful force that exists once a group is formed and produces significant behaviour.

Systems thinking looks at the effects of the system of which we are part. Our earliest introduction to any kind of system is the family. Many coaches may find their lives have been affected by these early experiences of being part of a system. How could coming from a fragmented family affect later career choices? Or how could acceptance of the status quo within organisations contribute to choice of career? Or lead to a search to be independent of organisations and a desire to be self-employed and work independently? These are questions coaches might ask of themselves before working with coachees who work within organisations; very often, external coaches have deliberately left one system as they no longer want to be part of it. However, they secure work by coaching people who still earn their living being part of that system.

Just as we produce particular behaviours within groups and are often held to those behaviours when we are part of a group, so too are we affected by the system of which a group is part. The systems we have been part of have formed our experiences and have in turn contributed to how we make sense of the world. Ignore the system and you ignore what will often determine successful coaching. Coaches unable to understand systems thinking can inadvertently and consistently encourage their coachees to leave one organisation to join another, for example. Many well intentioned training initiatives set out to produce more effective performance and new ways of thinking by sending people out of the organisation to study and participate in development programmes. Upon returning to work, they often find that their efforts are sabotaged by the rest of the system that hasn't either bought into the new way of thinking, or has felt excluded and continues as it is until the 'outsiders' are assimilated .

Coaching always results in an action but is preceded by thought, discussion and reflection.

Kolb's learning cycle[3] is one of the most well known and widely used concepts in training and development. It deals with the importance of being able to think about possibilities, try them out and then reflect on what worked, what didn't work and how it might be improved by thinking about what you want, trying it out and then thinking about what worked (reflecting) and so on. This reflective practice is something which benefits everyone, but often, especially in the workplace, the task in hand is so compelling that pausing to reflect is something that simply does not happen.

One of the most frequently given pieces of feedback to a coach is that the coachee hugely appreciated being given 'permission', and a confidential space, in which to reflect on his or her activities. Again, this is a behavioural process which coaching brings to the attention of people who otherwise may not have considered it.

UNDERSTANDING THE CHALLENGES OF COACHING

Experience suggests that there are two broad types of challenge faced by executive coaches.

- **First, there are the familiar and frequently encountered leadership challenges which executives often face. These typically include, for example, a crisis of confidence, a fear of being 'found out', or simply the difficulties associated with succeeding in a new role.**
- **The second type of challenge is altogether more daunting: it's the tricky type of situation that can leave even the most experienced coaches struggling outside their comfort zone. For instance, what should be done if coachees burst into tears? Or if they are dismissive, unable to see the big picture, inclined to ramble or veer off at a tangent, seem out of control, or simply don't know what they want to talk about?**

---

3   Kolb, D. A. *Experiential Learning Experience As a Source of Learning and Development.* Prentice-Hall, 1984.

We call these *typical challenges* and *difficult challenges*. The way to succeed with both types is clear. For the first category (the typical, familiar challenges) coaches need to perceive the issues correctly by using standard coaching processes and techniques, notably with intelligent, probing questions that enhance understanding and inform the coachees' thinking. The second type of challenge can be handled with experience, confidence and respect. Knowing how to manage yourself and your own emotional responses is essential in these situations.

Several skills are vitally important for both challenges: for example, self-awareness, calmness, patience, self-confidence and empathy. Also vitally important for both challenges, however, is knowing the right technique or approach to take at the right time. Explaining which technique works best in any given situation (or type of situation) is the focus of the next two sections.

However, before looking at specific techniques, it's important to remember that listening and holding a safe, supportive and non-judgemental space for coachees can sometimes be the only 'technique' required to help those individuals achieve their goals.

PART TWO

TYPICAL CHALLENGES FOR COACHES

People encounter a wide range of challenges in their working lives and these are often presented to executive coaches. Interestingly, while the specific details, pressures and contexts may vary enormously, many of the issues are, at their core, remarkably similar.

This section highlights some of the challenges that, in our experience, tend to be presented to coaches most often. Some are fiercely daunting and complex, some are vital but simple, but all of them are important – and getting the right approach is essential.

As a result, this section also suggests techniques that coaches can apply to help address these challenges.

The techniques listed against each challenge here are considered in detail in Part 5.

CLIENTS WORRY ABOUT 'BEING FOUND OUT'

Executives can often focus on their priorities or their team without actually appreciating how rare and valuable their skills are, or how good they are at what they do. Of course, there are many other executives who've no shortage of hubris or ego and who consider themselves superb, at least, for most of the time. Whatever the reality of their situation, several points are clear about clients who worry about being 'found out' (i.e. having a perceived lack of expertise or ability uncovered by someone else, usually their manager or a member of their team). In particular:

- **executives feel insecure and worried about their own competence – in which case, is this reasonable?**
- **executives value their own personal effectiveness and success – they're serious about doing well. The issue for the coach is how to build on this desire for self-awareness, improvement and success.**

POSSIBLE QUESTIONS

What evidence do the executives have to support this feeling? Why do they feel this way? What's the worst that could happen? Often, there may simply be a gap between where the clients' skills, knowledge or experience are at the moment, and where they need to be. In which case, how can this gap be managed? Would greater openness or honesty help? What can the individual do to redress the issue (if there is one) and would an action plan help?

USEFUL TOOLS AND TECHNIQUES

- **Transcending limiting beliefs**
- **Reframing**
- **Visualisation and future orientation**
- **Setting objectives and SMART goals**
- **Prioritising and managing your time**
- **360-degree feedback**
- **Developing business relationships**
- **Decision-making principles and techniques**
- **Circles of excellence**

CLIENTS WANT TO COMMUNICATE BETTER WITH COLLEAGUES

Communication is one of the pillars on which a senior executive's success rests. In fact, strong, engaging and inspiring communications can often help make a success of the most ordinary situations or strategies. One of the difficulties, however, is that leaders rarely get feedback on their communication style, and unless they are very self-aware they may not know whether – or how – to improve.

One point is especially important to remember: communication is *two-way*. Leaders need to listen at least as much as they need to explain.

Issues of communication can be tricky enough but when combined with other issues they can form a daunting obstacle. For example, colleagues may be in different offices, belong to a different culture, have a different history or experience, feel intensely competitive or sceptical, or simply not know each other. Despite these challenges, the old truth remains: communication is one of the pillars on which a senior executive's success rests.

POSSIBLE QUESTIONS

What are the obstacles to communication or what are the issues the executives need to resolve? For example, are the challenges related to distance, culture, past events or something else? What do you, as a coach, need to explain and what things do you need to know about? What can you do to build productive, proactive relationships – and with whom should these be? Are you connecting with the client at the right level – for example, are you talking about values and intangible issues to an intensely practical person? What communication techniques would work best? For example, could technology help? How will you know when communication improves – what will happen?

USEFUL TOOLS AND TECHNIQUES
- The Myers-Briggs Type indicator (MBTI)
- Fundamental interpersonal orientation (FIRO-B)
- GROW
- Inspiring trust

- The meta-mirror
- Questioning
- The four stages of achieving emotional commitment
- Logical levels
- Managing cross-cultural relationships and behaviour
- Developing business relationships
- Defusing tensions (acknowledge, ask, answer)

A CLIENT HAS RECENTLY BEEN APPOINTED TO A SENIOR POSITION

First-time appointees to a senior position face several major challenges. The first one being that it's the first time this has happened to them! These include understanding how they can best make their contribution; finding their 'place' and supporting other senior team-members, and taking a broad, strategic view rather than a narrow, parochial or technical one. Other complications include the team's size and history; the challenges that are faced and the quality of overall leadership. The key to success divides, broadly speaking, into two areas: helping the executives to understand how they can personally make the best contribution, and helping them define and recognise the team's priorities.

POSSIBLE QUESTIONS

What do executives need to know in order to feel differently? What are the team's priorities? What are the strengths and weaknesses? What expectations might people have of the client as a new team-member? Ask the client the following questions: What expectations do you have? Are these views (yours and others) clear and reasonable? What qualities do you bring to the team? How will you influence and persuade other senior colleagues of your views? What skills do you need to improve? What are your goals in the short term and long term? How will you measure success for the board and for you personally?

USEFUL TOOLS AND TECHNIQUES

- GROW
- Succeeding in a new job

- Developing influence (the Thomas-Kilmann Conflict Instrument)
- Visualisation and future orientation
- The balanced scorecard
- Setting objectives and SMART goals
- Kotter's eight-stage process for leading change
- Thinking strategically
- Developing business relationships
- Decision-making principles and techniques
- The meta-mirror
- Inspiring trust
- Six thinking hats
- Questioning
- Avoiding active inertia and moving from good to great
- Visualisation and future orientation

THE CLIENT IS UNSURE ABOUT WHERE TO START WITH THEIR ISSUES

Starting a new role or facing a rising tide of challenges or opportunities are common challenges for executives, and coaches are frequently asked for their support. The key is to decide whether to look *outward* – for example, setting the priorities for specific tasks, teams and individuals, or *inward*, with an emphasis on enhancing personal effectiveness.

POSSIBLE QUESTIONS

Before getting started and finding the best place to start, it's worth the coach asking *why* the client is unsure. For example, are they feeling insecure and if so, why? How can this be countered? The task of identifying the best place to start can be relatively straightforward – what are the priorities and options and which of these are most attractive, and why?

USEFUL TOOLS AND TECHNIQUES

- Force field analysis
- GROW
- Miracle question

- Succeeding in a new job
- Reframing
- Visualisation and future orientation
- Setting objectives and SMART goals
- Prioritising and managing your time
- Problem solving
- Decision-making principles and techniques
- Six thinking hats
- Scenario thinking

THE CLIENT IS UNCERTAIN ABOUT WHAT THEY WANT

There are many reasons why clients may be unsure about what they want. The coach's challenge is to help the clients to appreciate the causes of this uncertainty, as well as helping them to decide what they want. The temptation is to rush to find priorities and certainty, when what may be needed first is a clearer understanding of the causes of uncertainty. Revisiting the 'G' stage of the GROW model is a very useful thing to do at intervals during the coaching relationship.

POSSIBLE QUESTIONS

What is your current situation? Why are you uncertain about your options or the best way forward? When did this lack of certainty begin, and why? The next questions can then follow from the GROW model or other techniques: What are your goals? What matters to you and what do you enjoy? In an ideal world, what would you like? What do you want?

USEFUL TOOLS AND TECHNIQUES

- Miracle question
- GROW
- Questioning
- Force field analysis
- Setting objectives and SMART goals

■ Career development planning
■ Well-formed outcomes

CLIENTS CAN'T RELATE TO (OR DON'T WORK WELL WITH) THEIR BOSS OR COLLEAGUES

Many people's relationships are good: it's usually in everyone's interests for this to be the case, and individuals are essentially social beings. Yet it's precisely this contrast with the desired and valued norm of good relationships, combined with people's desire to be liked, valued or at least recognised, that makes weak relationships so stressful and unpleasant. And whilst many have good relationships, it's also the case that most people encounter difficult relationships at some time, and work, family or school are often where this happens. That's because in a free life we can usually choose our friends and the people we associate with – except in those circumstances.

It's also worth noting that in the late 20th and early 21st centuries, we've experienced an explosion in globalisation and the free movement of people, goods and services. We're now mixing more than ever with people from different cultures, experiences or generations. This brings a new perspective to a perennial issue. Improving relationships with people from your own culture or experience is one thing; improving them with people from a wholly different background can be something quite different.

The solution is, to begin with, an understanding that relationships are two-way and then move on to find out:

■ the causes of the weak (or non-existent) relationship;
■ the implications and effects of this situation;
■ possible options for: a) resolving differences, enhancing mutual understanding and improving the situation, or b) circumventing the difficulties, effectively 'ring-fencing' the problem so that a sustainable modus operandi can be established that lets both sides function without always encountering problems.

Finally, it can help to think about *intent*, both of the clients and their colleagues. This may help either to reduce or remove concerns, or else to crystallise legitimate grievances.

POSSIBLE QUESTIONS

What are the problems? What happens and how does this make you feel? How do you think they feel? What have been the results or consequences? What are the implications for the future (might this situation simply resolve itself)? What are your intentions and priorities? What are the other side's intentions or motivations? What are your options? What is your ideal? What, specifically, has happened for you to form this opinion?

USEFUL TOOLS AND TECHNIQUES

- **Miracle question**
- **GROW**
- **Questioning**
- **The meta-mirror**
- **Logical levels**
- **Defusing tensions (acknowledge, ask, answer)**
- **Inspiring trust**
- **Managing stress**
- **The Myers-Briggs type indicator (MBTI)**
- **Developing influence (the Thomas-Kilmann conflict instrument)**
- **Fundamental interpersonal relations orientation (FIRO-B)**
- **Managing cross-cultural relationships and behaviour**
- **Managing different generations**
- **Leading leaders**

NEW TEAM, FAST RESULTS

At some point a leader will usually take on a new team – and results are invariably needed quickly (whether or not the team itself is new). Several issues are especially significant: building and empowering the team, setting a clear direction, enabling people to succeed and, once this is happening, building on their success.

POSSIBLE QUESTIONS

What are your priorities? What are the team's objectives and what is the timescale? What is your vision or direction? What will success look like? What are the team's strengths? What skills need to be enhanced and how will this happen? What are the potential weaknesses or pitfalls facing the team and how will these be countered? What resources do you need to secure for the team?

USEFUL TOOLS AND TECHNIQUES

- GROW
- Kotter's eight-stage process for leading change
- Prioritising and managing your time
- Eight principles of motivation
- Empowerment
- The balanced scorecard
- The four stages of achieving emotional commitment
- Avoiding active inertia and moving from good to great
- Developing innovation
- Decision-making principles and techniques
- Inspiring trust
- The Myers-Briggs type indicator (MBTI)
- Visualisation and future orientation
- Succeeding in a new job
- Setting objectives and SMART goals
- Action-centred leadership
- Leadership styles
- Six thinking hats
- Teamworking (Belbin's team types)

NEED TO HAVE A TOUGH CONVERSATION

Two clichés are particularly worth remembering in this situation. First, managers do things right, but leaders do the right thing. Second, leadership is not a popularity contest. Sometimes, the truth of these maxims means that leaders need to have a difficult conversation with someone. What usually matters is that when your clients have to do this, they display:

- **empathy** – understanding how the other person feels;
- **fairness** – in particular, the ability to do the right thing and retain the moral high ground;
- **openness and honesty** – being open and transparent about their intentions, why they're doing what needs to be done.

This can also help clients to maintain a clear focus on the benefits of the conversation.

POSSIBLE QUESTIONS

Why is this conversation going to be difficult? How can you make it easier for the other person (and, as a result, for you)? Are you being reasonable? What are your intentions? How can you support the other person? Would it help to have evidence or additional support when you have the conversation? When will you speak with the other person – what is the best time or setting? What will be the best outcome from this conversation? What are the facts versus what are the subjective/emotional judgements?

USEFUL TOOLS AND TECHNIQUES

- **Fundamental interpersonal relations orientation (FIRO-B)**
- **Logical levels**
- **The meta-mirror**
- **Defusing tensions (acknowledge, ask, answer)**
- **Problem solving**
- **Managing stress**
- **Managing cross-cultural relationships and behaviour**
- **Managing different generations**
- **Developing influence (the Thomas-Kilmann conflict instrument)**

DIFFICULTIES MANAGING TIME OR ACHIEVING A WORK–LIFE BALANCE

The greatest pressure often comes from within – the fears or pressures that people exert on themselves – rather than from others. So, is the pressure real or imagined? What's the worst that could happen? Time pressures can often lead to stress, with consequences for one's personal life. What matters is the ability to agree realistic priorities and then focus on these, as well as the ability to delegate, renegotiate or delay other tasks. The ability to secure additional resources may also be valuable.

POSSIBLE QUESTIONS

What do you want? What's stopping you achieving your goals? How do you spend your time? Are the issues related to too many tasks, too few resources, too little time, too few skills, or are they simply 'unwinnable' tasks? In an ideal world, how would your work and home life look? What practical steps can you take to achieve this? Whose support do you need? What practical steps can you take to resolve or improve the situation? What is your preferred timescale?

USEFUL TOOLS AND TECHNIQUES

- **Achieving a sense of purpose**
- **Transcending limiting beliefs**
- **Balancing work and personal life**
- **Questioning**
- **Miracle question**
- **Career development planning**
- **GROW**
- **Managing stress**

CLIENTS HAVE RECENTLY ARRIVED FROM SOMEWHERE COMPLETELY DIFFERENT – WHAT SHOULD THEY DO HERE?

In a commercial context, the answer to this deceptively difficult question can lie in several places. Find out what the clients think needs to be done first – what are the most significant priorities, challenges or opportunities? What does their manager want them to do? What would the shareholders expect them to do? What do their customers want? And finally, what do their colleagues want? Colleagues can often shout loudest, so while it may pay to listen to their advice, it can also be useful to keep an independent mind.

Also important is the need to balance short-term gains with longer-term objectives. In fact, the question 'what should I do here?' can be answered at several levels: this week, this month, this quarter, this year, or over the next three years. Illustrating this point is an apocryphal story concerning a TV station in Washington DC. It was Christmas Eve and the local TV news anchor was just closing their programme. He said: 'We asked the ambassadors of three local embassies what they most wanted this Christmas. The French ambassador said he wanted peace, security and an end to conflict and suffering. The German ambassador replied that he wanted global economic growth, financial stability and greater prosperity. And the British ambassador replied that he wanted a box of crystallised fruit.' Clearly, it helps to adopt the right perspective at the right time.

POSSIBLE QUESTIONS

What are your expectations of the role and what are the expectations of others? How do they differ? What is your timescale? What do you think you can achieve? What would you like to do? What do you think is achievable in the short and longer term? What aspects of your experience are most useful? What happened to your predecessor? What are the expectations of your boss, shareholders and customers? Where is the low-hanging fruit? How can you generate momentum or quick wins? What is your long-term vision for yourself, your team and your business?

USEFUL TOOLS AND TECHNIQUES

- Force field analysis
- Questioning
- Miracle question
- Career development planning
- Scenario thinking
- Reframing
- GROW
- Kotter's eight-stage process for leading change
- Prioritising and managing your time
- Thinking strategically
- The balanced scorecard
- The four stages of achieving emotional commitment
- Avoiding active inertia and moving from good to great
- Developing innovation
- The decision-making process
- Decision-making principles and techniques
- Inspiring trust
- The Myers-Briggs type indicator (MBTI)
- Visualisation and future orientation
- Succeeding in a new job
- Setting objectives and SMART goals
- Action-centred leadership
- Teach me

THE CLIENT IS DEALING WITH GUILT

People make mistakes. What matters is having the ability to recognise a mistake, even a bad one, for what it is, and having the desire to prevent it recurring and move on. We can't change the past, so if we've dealt with the past and developed positive plans for the future then that's the most that can be expected.

With guilt, it can help to talk about the past, learn the necessary lessons and then move on. It sounds easy but it can be very difficult to achieve. This is one of the most sensitive areas of coaching, and it may be the case that the professional support of a counsellor or therapist would be useful for the clients. Almost certainly, you as a coach will benefit from the support of your own supervisor in this situation.

POSSIBLE QUESTIONS

Ask your clients: Why do you feel guilty? What, specifically, do you feel guilty about? Is this reasonable? What can you do (or have you done) to rectify the situation? What have you learnt from the situation? Have you spoken to others who were also involved – what is their view? Who can you talk to about this issue? What are your plans and priorities for the future? What would be the best thing you could do?

USEFUL TOOLS AND TECHNIQUES

- **Transcending limiting beliefs**
- **Reframing**
- **The meta-mirror**
- **Managing stress**
- **Coaching supervision**
- **Mentoring**
- **The Myers-Briggs type indicator (MBTI)**

CLIENTS NEED TO BE MORE CREATIVE

Ideas and decisions are the footsteps of progress. In 'Scenario thinking' (see Part 4), we make the point that there are two things we know for certain about the future: it will be different and it will surprise. Being creative and capable of adjusting to new situations and opportunities, as well as challenges, is therefore essential. Everyone has the capacity to be creative; however, some people find it more difficult than others.

If a client expresses the need or desire to be more creative, there are several practical tools to help them stimulate their thinking. Edward de Bono's 'Six thinking hats', as well as other lateral thinking techniques, are well known in this area. Finally, there's a surprising link between coaching and innovating: that's the ability to 'question'. It's possible to generate new ideas and perceptions simply by asking questions such as: Why? Why not? What? How? Where? When? Who else might be involved?

POSSIBLE QUESTIONS

Why do you need to be creative? Where do you find you get stuck – for example, is it generating ideas personally or getting others to be more creative? Do you need to implement ideas, solve problems, or develop new products or processes? What resources do you have at your disposal?

USEFUL TOOLS AND TECHNIQUES

- Developing innovation
- Six thinking hats
- Force field analysis
- Questioning
- Miracle question
- Reframing
- Disney creativity strategy

THE CLIENT IS WORKING WITH PEOPLE FROM DIFFERENT CULTURES

HSBC, a leading financial services business, strives to be 'The world's local bank' and they have a clear, compelling view: 'In a world where a uniformity and standardisation dominate, we are building our business in the belief that different people from different cultures and different walks of life create value.'[1] In other words, people with different and varied combinations of skills and experiences are likely to be able to adopt a broader perspective and apply a broader range of skills than people from a single culture or experience.

One of the keys to success in this area is the ability for people to buy-in to a collective, shared vision of the future. Different perspectives need to be united around a single focus or purpose. Also important is the need to avoid stereotyping or generalising. People value their individuality – so should each of your clients.

---

1 HSBC, www.hsbc.com

POSSIBLE QUESTIONS

How easy is it to manage people from other cultures? What issues do you find arise, why, and how might these be resolved? What is it that unites you and what separates you? How can you channel the differences to greatest benefit or effect? How can you alter your behaviour to show understanding, empathy and respect? What is your ideal or vision for your cross-cultural relationships?

USEFUL TOOLS AND TECHNIQUES

- Inspiring trust
- Visualisation and future orientation
- Managing cross-cultural relationships and behaviour
- Logical levels
- Questioning

A CLIENT NEEDS TO BE MORE OF A 'PEOPLE PERSON'

Executives can often focus on 'hard' aspects of business, such as finance or processes, and neglect the softer aspects, such as the need to get the most from their people. People are invariably an organisation's most critical, expensive and decisive resource; products and processes may be copied and finance acquired but people's combinations of skills, behaviour and experience are unique. It's up to leaders to get the most from their people: helping the business achieve its full potential by helping its employees to achieve theirs. A useful way to make progress is for clients to understand the value of empathy, treating others as they would wish to be treated.

POSSIBLE QUESTIONS

Get your clients to tell you about their teams – what are their strengths and weaknesses? What are the priorities for the future, and what are the implications for team-members? What effect do you – as leader – have on your team? In what ways do you need to be more of a 'people person' – why, why now, and how do you want to achieve this? What will success look like? What does being a people person mean to you?

USEFUL TOOLS AND TECHNIQUES

- The Myers-Briggs Type indicator (MBTI)
- Fundamental interpersonal relations orientation (FIRO-B)
- Developing business relationships
- Inspiring trust
- The meta-mirror
- Managing cross-cultural relationships and behaviour
- Logical levels
- Defusing tensions (acknowledge, ask, answer)
- Managing different generations
- Eight principles of motivation
- Enhancing motivation
- Empowerment
- Developing influence (the Thomas-Kilmann conflict instrument)
- GROW
- The four stages of achieving emotional commitment
- Setting objectives and SMART goals
- Action-centred leadership
- Leadership styles
- Teamworking (Belbin's team types)
- Mentoring
- Coaching supervision
- Leading leaders

CLIENTS WANT TO MAINTAIN THEIR MOTIVATION

Anyone can become demotivated. The key to success is to recognise this situation, understand why it's happening, decide what it is that you're looking for and then take practical steps to get there. This needs to happen swiftly because a lack of motivation is corrosive and can quickly become damaging for the client and their colleagues. It is a serious situation requiring self-awareness and the ability to take prompt, effective action to get back on track.

POSSIBLE QUESTIONS

Why are you demotivated – what are the causes? What are the effects or consequences of this? In an ideal world, how would things be different? What can you do to improve the situation today, this week, this month?

USEFUL TOOLS AND TECHNIQUES

- **GROW**
- **Problem solving**
- **Achieving a sense of purpose**
- **Balancing work and personal life**
- **Eight principles of motivation**
- **Enhancing motivation**
- **Career development planning**
- **Prioritising and managing your time**
- **Transcending limiting beliefs**
- **Managing stress**
- **Coaching supervision**
- **Mentoring**
- **The Myers-Briggs type indicator (MBTI)**

CLIENTS WANT TO DEVELOP THEIR CAREER

The best leaders invariably look for new challenges or ways to keep their skills up to date. It's also the case that talented people often (but not always) look to develop their career, not only for the rewards it brings in terms of remuneration and recognition but also because of their desire for new challenges, stimulation and opportunity.

Several general points are worth remembering. First, career planning needs careful consideration and benefits from discussion with the people that know the clients best – their family, friends and colleagues. Second, structuring a career development plan can benefit from a personal profile: this will help the clients to understand their skills, experience, strengths and weaknesses, and then match these with the challenges they envisage – both now and in the future.

The starting point is to develop a plan and this typically includes the following elements.

- **Situational analysis** ('Where are you now?'). This should include career details to date such as job roles and the highlights and challenges of each role. Also include a short overview of the common themes from job roles, highlighting knowledge and experience (e.g. marketing or retailing), specific skills (e.g. project management or marketing) and capabilities that are valued by the organisation.
- **Personal objectives** ('Where do you want to be?'). Write your personal vision for the next 5–10 years (e.g. achieving a particular role by a certain time). Outline the knowledge, skills and capabilities required for that role and how they'll be attained. Also, decide how progress towards your vision will be measured – the milestones along your way. What are the success criteria?
- **Strategy** ('How are you going to get there?'). Target specific interim roles that will provide the knowledge and skills needed to take on the 'vision' role and set a timeframe for interim roles.
- **Consider constraints and dependencies.** Plan to resolve or overcome any obstacles (personal or professional) to achieving your desired outcome.
- **Take action.** It's each individual's responsibility to implement a personal action plan. They should include details of: development objectives, planned activities, details of when they will be completed, any support needed and when progress will be reviewed. Also, be clear about how the results will be integrated into the workplace.
- **Current reality check.** Is this ambition relevant today or is it one that was fixed on a number of years ago and which has not been revisited or re-evaluated in the context of the present?

POSSIBLE QUESTIONS

- What are your motives and priorities for development? How do they fit with your business's strategy and objectives?
- What are your strengths and weaknesses – what should you be doing better, what future challenges are you likely to encounter? How do you know these strengths and weaknesses are as you think they are?
- Who will support your learning and development? What resources or opportunities are available to you?
- Do you have a current personal development plan?
- What do you need to improve and how will you apply what you have learnt? How will you assess and measure your progress?

A personal profile can be created by considering the following.

- **Priorities.** What really matters to you personally? Do you know what sort of leader you want to be? Who are your role models and why did they succeed?
- **Work experience.** What positions have you held? When did you succeed and why? How could your performance have been better?
- **Achievements.** What have been your greatest achievements? What gave you greatest pleasure and what impressed others?
- **Personal attitudes and style.** Assessing how you behave in different situations can help you to understand the way you feel and behave: where you are likely to be strong and when you might feel less certain. For example: do you become energised around people or do you prefer to spend time alone? Do you think quickly or do you tend to take time to reflect before speaking? Do you do a few things well or do you prefer to pursue many opportunities superficially? Are you an open person or more private? Do you prefer order and structure or do you tend to live spontaneously, remaining open to possibilities?

USEFUL TOOLS AND TECHNIQUES

■ Career development planning

■ Succeeding in a new job

■ Setting objectives and SMART goals

■ Achieving a sense of purpose

■ Transcending limiting beliefs

■ Balancing work and personal life

■ The leadership pipeline

■ Miracle question

■ 360-degree feedback

STRUGGLING TO DEAL WITH CHANGE

As has already been said, there are two things we can say for certain about the future: it will be different and it will surprise. People often value familiarity and consistency or, to view it another way, people fear uncertainty. This fear is often a significant reason why people struggle to cope with change. Crucially, at the heart of their fear often lies concern or insecurity about a loss of control. This leads people to resist or resent change and to feel stressed.

The solution is to help clients understand *how* and *why* they feel the way they do, and help them think about what practical action they can take to improve their situation.

POSSIBLE QUESTIONS

If this situation was solved, what would the solution look like? How can we build on the pluses? How can we eliminate the minuses? What ideas can we borrow, adapt or combine? Where are the potential pitfalls and how could these be overcome? What is your role in the new situation – what would improve your situation and how can this be achieved?

USEFUL TOOLS AND TECHNIQUES

■ The meta-mirror

■ Logical levels

■ Reframing

- Transcending limiting beliefs
- Miracle question
- Questioning
- GROW
- Developing influence (the Thomas-Kilmann conflict instrument)
- Kotter's eight-stage process for leading change
- Problem solving
- Managing stress
- The four stages of achieving emotional commitment
- Six thinking hats

FEELING LONELY AT THE TOP

Leadership is synonymous with consistency and moral courage. Although this may mean different things to different people at various times, it does imply an ability to do and say what you mean, especially when faced with adversity. Moral courage also requires a capacity to take risks, to be constant and determined, to admit mistakes and to stand alone when necessary. For this reason, it can be lonely at the top. It's worth noting, however, that courage is a quality that's universally respected; even if a particular idea or approach isn't agreed upon, bravery and associated qualities of integrity, conviction and determination tend to be admired.

So, while leadership isn't a popularity contest, it isn't an *unpopularity* contest either – meaning that to get things done invariably requires sound judgement, empathy, influence and support. These can be diminished by feelings of isolation and loneliness and it's important, therefore, for these feelings to be overcome.

Broadly speaking, potential solutions come in two varieties: first, exploring and addressing the reasons why individuals feels lonely, and what lonely means to them; second, helping them to connect with sources of information or support.

POSSIBLE QUESTIONS

Why do you feel this way? Is it reasonable or unreasonable, deserved or not, temporary or longer-term? How do you want things to change? What are the priorities for action in the short and long term, for the business, the team and each individual? What is the reality of your situation and what are your options? What will success look like? How will you measure success?

USEFUL TOOLS AND TECHNIQUES

- Succeeding in a new job
- Setting objectives and SMART goals
- Achieving a sense of purpose
- Prioritising and managing your time
- Developing business relationships
- Inspiring trust
- The Myers-Briggs type indicator (MBTI)
- Fundamental interpersonal relations orientation (FIRO-B)
- Mentoring
- Transcending limiting beliefs
- Miracle question
- GROW

DEALING WITH DIFFERENT GENERATIONS

The renowned management thinker, Peter Drucker, writing in *The Economist* in November 2001, pointed out that: 'In a knowledge economy, there are no such things as conscripts – there are only volunteers. The trouble is we have trained our managers to manage conscripts.' This situation is highlighted by the challenge of managing people from generations other than your own. In fact, in recent years workforces have changed dramatically. For example, talented employees are emerging from a much wider range of countries than ever before.

Also, the range of skills needed is more varied and the nature of the workplace is more complex. It used to be that the old were in charge of the young, who did what they were told. That situation is now eroding and one of the keys to engaging employees at work is to understand the generational divide. Several techniques are useful.

- **Segment your approach and accommodate each generation's perspective.** There are different groups in the workforce and members of each generation have their own motivators, attributes and preferences resulting from the formative events and conditions that they shared. Common experience doesn't always dictate common attitudes among a particular generation, but it can mean that people tend to carry similar influences throughout their careers.

- **Recognise the limitations of your own experience.** Your own experience as a manager is important but it has been shaped by both your own personal experiences and those of your generation. Another person of another generation may well have a completely different set of priorities, values, concerns and preferences. Thinking back to what you wanted may take you in the wrong direction. Also, remember that, in a world where homogeneity and standardisation dominate, it's the combination of different people, and the fusion of different ideas, that provides the essential fuel for progress and success.

- **Be flexible when you interview or promote people.** If you stick rigidly to a prescriptive job description or set of capabilities, then you may end up missing a gem. Find out what people can do as well as what they can't, and be flexible.

- **Understand that many of today's employees don't respond to traditional motivators.** This points to the need for a different approach. For example, be prepared to discuss what people want and value – don't always assume that, based on your own experience, you already know what's required. Also, be prepared to use different techniques and styles when communicating. The manager who views engaging, motivating and rewarding people as an exciting challenge will be amongst the best of managers.

■ **Empathise and look past the clutter.** This means learning from others but also understanding that engaging people requires a customised approach. This comes from an open dialogue based around two issues: first, what can I do for you? Second, here's what I need from you.

POSSIBLE QUESTIONS

What do people want? What are their motives and 'drivers'? What are the formative experiences of the people in your team? Are you relating to people as individuals? Do you find it difficult to flex or shed your views of the way things should be done? Could – and should – you show greater flexibility? What are the strengths of other generations and how can you get the greatest benefit from them?

USEFUL TOOLS AND TECHNIQUES

■ **Logical levels**
■ **Enhancing motivation**
■ **Empowerment**
■ **Managing different generations**
■ **Leadership styles**
■ **Developing business relationships**
■ **Inspiring trust**
■ **The Myers-Briggs type indicator (MBTI)**
■ **Fundamental interpersonal relations orientation (FIRO-B)**
■ **Questioning**
■ **GROW**
■ **Developing influence (the Thomas-Kilmann conflict instrument)**
■ **Teamworking (Belbin's team types)**

CLIENTS LACK CONFIDENCE, SELF-ESTEEM, SKILLS OR ABILITY, OR FEEL THEY'RE TOO YOUNG OR TOO OLD (OR ANY OTHER SPECIFIC LIMITING BELIEFS)

One obvious point about life is often forgotten, especially by people who are immersed in important or absorbing work or who are influential, highly driven or ambitious. It's that there are always things in life we can do well, *and there are always things in life that we will be unable to do well or at all*. So, for example, as writers and coaches we three authors of this book may feel quite confident, whereas if we were playing in the midfield for Real Madrid we would, quite possibly, be less sure of ourselves (although probably not as uncertain as our fellow team-mates would feel!). The point is to develop self-awareness, accurately understanding what we can do, what we cannot do, and what we can achieve with further preparation and action.

This challenge may have several interrelated elements for clients. For example, they may feel this way because:

- **they've set themselves high (or possibly unrealistic) standards and expectations;**
- **they've been set unrealistic expectations by others;**
- **they fear a loss of influence or control, possibly because they're new to a role or situation;**
- **they feel inferior or uncertain in relation to others around them.**

As their coach, your challenge is to help clients discover why they feel this way, ask them to assess whether these feelings are reasonable (and specifically which feelings are reasonable), and encourage them to develop a plan to resolve or improve the situation.

Discussing and exploring the client's feelings is a powerful place to start and it may help to point out several simple truths. For example, confidence can be increased with practical action, skills can be learnt or acquired, and issues of age change with time and anyway are becoming much less significant in the workplace.

POSSIBLE QUESTIONS

Ask your clients: why do you feel this way? Is it reasonable – what objective evidence do you have for your view (e.g. that you lack adequate skills)? What are the consequences (what is the worst that could happen)? When did you first have this view? Is it caused by an isolated incident or is it a broader, more legitimate issue? What are your strengths, weaknesses and areas for development? How did this situation develop or emerge? How would you like things to be? What can you do to improve your position?

USEFUL TOOLS AND TECHNIQUES

- **Miracle question**
- **GROW**
- **The meta-mirror**
- **Reframing**
- **Transcending limiting beliefs**
- **Logical levels**
- **Succeeding in a new job**
- **Defusing tensions (acknowledge, ask, answer)**

CONTRACTING

Contracting simply means agreeing with the client (the individual being coached) and, where appropriate, the employing organisation or higher authority, arrangements and ground rules for your work as coach. Contracting is simple but essential and it's one of the cornerstones of professional coaching.

There are two common areas of difficulty with contracting. First, the coach may not feel comfortable or confident formally agreeing 'rules' – it could get in the way of rapport and other important, early-stage activities. Second, your natural enthusiasm and desire to focus on the client may mean you rush through contracting or ignore it altogether. Both are understandable but neither is acceptable: contracting is a vital and indispensable part of coaching. The solution is for coaches to:

- consider their ground rules in advance of the coaching session;
- agree with the client (and their employer, where appropriate) the terms of their coaching work. This covers such issues as confidentiality, timing and frequency of sessions, the purpose of the coaching intervention, and any other general issues of significance to the people involved;
- stick to the agreed contract!

Finally, as with the next challenge, it can positively help coaches if they show professionalism with a desire to establish a framework or contract for their coaching intervention. This also helps establish confidence and credibility – another reason, therefore, why contracting is valuable.

POSSIBLE QUESTIONS

Let me explain how I normally work...is this all right? Can I suggest we agree to organise sessions as follows...? What results do you want to see from the coaching session? What are your priorities?

USEFUL TOOLS AND TECHNIQUES

- Miracle question
- GROW
- Logical levels
- Questioning

SELLING YOURSELF AS A COACH

This challenge requires confidence and self-awareness. It's tempting to ask: if you find this task difficult then how effective will you really be as a coach – especially if you're working with senior executives? This is because coaches need to develop their confidence and self-awareness before anything else, so they'll work well with other people. In this way, selling yourself is great preparation for the direct, honest and open conversations that you'll probably need from time to time as an executive coach.

The solution, therefore, is to plan your approach, prepare and develop your confidence by being clear about what you have to offer.

POSSIBLE QUESTIONS

There are several useful questions that coaches can consider in advance of coaching assignments. For example: Why should anyone be coached by you? What makes you qualified to be a coach? What do you have to offer? Why should people work with you and not someone else – what makes you unique? Can you justify your fees?

USEFUL TOOLS AND TECHNIQUES

- Developing business relationships
- Reframing
- Transcending limiting beliefs
- Inspiring trust
- Questioning
- GROW
- Developing influence (the Thomas-Kilmann conflict instrument)

TIME-KEEPING AND ENDING A COACHING SESSION

It can be difficult, awkward or even inappropriate to end a coaching session simply because the allotted time has been reached. This is particularly true when ideas, energy or emotion are in full flow. Also, it can also be a challenge simply to keep clients 'on track' and engaged, thinking clearly and productively on their issues. Sometimes it seems that no sooner has this started than the session runs out of time. Precisely how these issues are resolved largely depends on the coach's personal style although openness is always advisable. Several other points are relevant.

- Preparation by the clients is invaluable: considering their issues in advance can help to get them straight into the substantive coaching discussion soon after the session begins.

■ During the session the coach needs to keep an eye on how things are progressing and, if necessary, periodically give information about the time remaining, rather than bringing the session to an abrupt and surprising close.

■ The coach should check progress with the client – it may be the case that while the coach feels progress is slow, the client may be finding the session revelatory and invaluable!

■ Where possible (and where appropriate), it's often useful for the coach to give the client work to do between sessions (or after the session if only one conversation is planned).

■ If timekeeping is noticed to be an issue for clients (i.e. they are regularly late for appointments, or want to finish early), then this might be something to reflect back to them, in relation to whether it's a feature of problems they're having outside the coaching relationship.

POSSIBLE QUESTIONS

How are we doing for time? Are we making progress? Do you we think we'll cover all the issues today? What should we focus on now and what can agree to cover at another time (either in the next session or by the client after the session)?

USEFUL TOOLS AND TECHNIQUES

■ GROW
■ Setting objectives and SMART goals
■ Prioritising and managing your time
■ They Myers-Briggs type indicator (MBTI)

CLIENTS NEED TO THINK LONG TERM AND PLAN FOR THE FUTURE

Among the defining characteristics of a successful leader is an ability to balance detail and a big picture view, as well as handling immediate pressures and a longer-term perspective simultaneously. This is especially challenging as the pressures of modern life and work invariably demand immediate attention. How, then, can a coach help their client to keep these two potentially conflicting priorities in balance? There are several possible answers.

First, short-term and long-term or detail and big picture decisions may not be in conflict at all, just different parts of a continuum. In this case, short-term decisions can be used to support longer-term goals, and vice versa.

Second, it can help to view different issues as equal priorities overall, but they may assume special significance at particular moments. Think of it like a child's seesaw: one moment one side is in the ascendancy (e.g. short-term issues), the next moment it is the other side (long-term issues). What matters is that progress is made on both fronts over time, *but not necessarily simultaneously*.

POSSIBLE QUESTIONS

The challenge of focusing on the long term instead of immediate pressures can be achieved in several ways, as outlined below – these apply to individuals, teams or organisations.

- **Visualisation and strategic thinking.** This involves standing back from the day-to-day routine and taking a longer-term perspective. What do you want to achieve? What is your plan (or strategy) for moving from where are you now to where you want to be? What resources or skills do you need to make progress?
- **Scenarios.** Scenarios are perspectives on potential events and their consequences, providing a context in which managers can make decisions. Scenarios help managers tackle risk, uncertainty and complexity. Scenario planning enables organisations to rehearse the future, to walk the battlefield before battle commences so that they're better prepared. Their value lies not in a prediction of the future, but in their ability to recognise and understand future developments, enabling managers to influence events.

  Ask your clients: do you think actively about the future? What are the main issues, challenges, opportunities and priorities? Do you understand how different circumstances could affect your business in the future? Does your organisation encourage creativity and debate when discussing the future? Do you construct scenarios formally – building models and assigning each a different probability – or informally – using them merely as a base to guide sensible actions?

- **Resource thinking.** There are three main problems with existing approaches to leading and growing a business and implementing strategy. First, businesses are often backward looking, relying on established success formulas and (at least subconsciously) believing 'If it ain't broke, don't fix it.' Second, businesses focus on the present: the next quarter's results, the daily fluctuations of the stock price. Finally, future projections and longer-term plans can be flawed, either plain wrong or else failing to take adequate account of variables, undermining the whole strategy.

The real weakness of existing approaches is that they're largely static, offering little explanation of what it is that's driving a firm's performance through time. They're also approximate, relying on sound leadership to make the course corrections. A better approach is to focus on resources: the factors driving success or failure. Success is determined by whether resources strengthen or decline, complement or undermine each other, take from competitors or are eroded by them.

People and teams are often capable of far more than they imagine; they need to understand the factors driving their success, to be able to piece together the elements needed and to choose objectives grounded in both reality and aspiration.

Why is performance following its current path? Where is it going if you carry on as you are? How can you design a robust strategy to radically improve performance in the future? How many resources do you have? How do they interact and affect each other? In particular, how do they affect the quantity and quality of other resources? Do you use people to build, develop, retain and use resources? Are you sure that your organisation is configured to do this as effectively as possible? Do you ensure that people enhance the quality of your resources?

USEFUL TOOLS AND TECHNIQUES
■ **Visualisation and future orientation**
■ **Scenario thinking**
■ **Career development planning**

GETTING THE RIGHT COACHING SUPERVISION

Coaching supervision is an opportunity for coaches to reflect on their work, with a trained coaching supervisor, either one-to-one or in a group. Peer supervision amongst a group of coaches can also be a useful source of supervision. Its primary purpose, reflection, is to understand better any challenging and complex situations and to gain more clarity going forward. Significantly, it's also an opportunity to receive practical support (e.g. ideas and suggestions) and emotional support. Finally, supervision can be invaluable as a way of ensuring ongoing learning and professional development and checking on boundary management.

The benefits of supervision include: educational development of coaches and the fulfilment of their potential; practical and psychological support; quality assurance and managerial excellence. Supervision benefits both coaches and their clients. Management by a supervisor ensures that coaches are working responsibly and to the best of their ability, and also ensures an informed check on quality and ethics. Good supervision also benefits the interests and well-being of coaches.

The supervisor shares with the coach responsibility for ensuring that the coach's work is professional, ethical and as successful as possible. The supervisor provides feedback or direction that will enable coaches to develop the skills, theoretical knowledge and personal attributes they need to succeed. Above all, the supervisor listens, provides support and challenges coaches whenever personal issues, questions, concerns or insecurities arise.

Most professional coaching bodies now have evidence of coaching supervision as a mandatory requirement of membership.

POSSIBLE QUESTIONS

How often is supervision necessary for me? Can I work well with my supervisor – do I like and respect the person? What are the priorities for me [the coach] when I am being supervised? What are the supervisor's strengths?

USEFUL TOOLS AND TECHNIQUES
■ **Coaching supervision**
■ **Reframing**
■ **Questioning**

PART THREE

DIFFICULT CHALLENGES FOR COACHES

This section looks at some of the most challenging, daunting and problematic issues presented to coaches. Some of these are commonplace, others less so, and all can present themselves in a wide variety of ways.

We suggest issues for coaches and their clients to consider, and highlight possible ways that each might be addressed. This is done in a coaching, questioning style, to prompt thoughts for coaches and so they can adapt the questions to their own particular coaching style.

The specific techniques to which we refer are described in Part 4.

Please note that the specific techniques to which we refer are described in detail in Part 4.

Difficult challenges for coaches	Issues to consider	Possible solutions
The client is defensive Define 'defensive' and take great care when using this term – it's a loaded word and issue. Usually, if you describe a behaviour to someone, you're likely to prompt that behaviour in them. So, if you say to individuals 'you seem defensive/angry/anxious', then their likely response will be defensive, angry or anxious!	• Is it a valid response? Is it justified? • Are you, the coach, producing the defensiveness? • Why are they defensive? • What evidence is there of defensiveness? • Is it temporary, deserved or longer-term? • Are issues of confidence and sensitivity at work? • What are the consequences of their defensiveness? • How can you reduce their defensive-ness and get them to be more open to advice and constructive? • Which option would work best: a) ignoring it and hoping things improve; b) gently confronting the issue; c) changing your approach and finding a way round their defensiveness? • Why does their defensiveness matter – what effect is it having?	• **Parallel process** – when you give feedback, explain to the client what you're observing and the response it's producing in you, their coach. • **Reframing or meta-mirror** – would it help the client to view the situation from a different perspective? • **Logical levels** – what's motivating the client? What's the lens through which they perceive the world? What are their priorities and guiding influences?
The client is behaving emotionally (e.g. feeling low, depressed or crying) Consider whether this is a valid response. Do you understand the client's situation and emotions? (Coaches often want to rush to solve problems and sometimes this isn't feasible – for example, in the case of bereavement.) If a client mentions depression, ask whether it's clinical or if they are receiving treatment for it. Many people seek medical treatment for this and other similar issues – is that the case here (if a client openly talks about being depressed)?	• Why is the client upset? • Would a 'time-out' help? Is this situation positive or negative? • Is this an opportunity? Emotion is sometimes accompanied by determination, energy and a clear focus – can these be channelled to help the client? • What are the immediate priorities for the client, and what longer-term goals would be of benefit?	• **Ask the client** what would help them the most in this session. • **Be flexible** and ask the client if this is the best time for the coaching session. • **Empathy** is always valuable and sympathy is sometimes appropriate. How can you best provide support? • **Miracle question** – what does the client want, and what do they want to change or improve?

Difficult challenges for coaches	Issues to consider	Possible solutions
The client is silent, uncommunicative or withdrawn	• Does the client know what is going to happen in this session and what to expect? • What evidence do you have for your view that the client is uncommunicative or withdrawn? • If this is a second or subsequent session, and the client was communicative in the first, explain your observation to the client and ask why there's a difference. • Check your perception – is this based on your observation or is it simply two different personality (see MBTI) types perceiving each other?	• Communicate: explain what you observe, provide evidence to support your view, ask for a response. • Consider what information you have about your client e.g. is this behaviour consistent with data from a Myers-Briggs type indicator (MBTI), Fundamental Interpersonal Relations Indicator (FIRO-B), or pre-coaching briefing – or is it happening for the first time? • Explain to the client why you are there, and what is possible within the session (what can be achieved).
The client is dismissive of you [the coach] or coaching, leadership or development	• This is the client's opinion and opinions are usually valid, within a range of experience. So, ask what experiences the client has had to validate this opinion. Why do they take this view? • The client will have criteria which will make your session worthwhile for them – so, find out what those criteria are.	• Acknowledge the client's right to have an opinion – it may be valid. Acknowledging the issue will also remove some of the 'personal sting' from the issue. • Ask the client what they need for it to be a worthwhile solution.
Outpourings The client has either raised a large number of issues, or raise a large number of significant points about an issue.	• Be prepared for an extroverted thinker to provide you with a great deal of information. • Be aware of your own personal preferences – if you coach as an introvert then there could be a feeling of too much information for you to deal with (see MBTI). • This can be a 'cathartic intervention' in itself (see Heron).	• Make notes. • Feed back to client the number of issues they've raised, then narrow them down by asking which three would be most important for the session. • Give them time to seriously say all that they need to say, then get on with the work.

Difficult challenges for coaches	Issues to consider	Possible solutions
Small chunk thinking The client is having difficulty seeing the big picture.	• Certain roles require small chunk thinking, whereas strategic roles require a broader perspective. So, this thinking style may be entirely reasonable and valid, or it may reflect a pattern of behaviour. • Also, it may be a preference (and would be highlighted by a profiling tool such as MBTI). • Everyone is capable of both big picture and small chunk thinking – the strength of their preference governs how easy or difficult it will be to do the opposite.	• Feed back to the clients what you observe. • Help them to practise. If necessary, lead them through each step of the process. • Use techniques involving 'visualisation' so that they can get a stronger picture of the overall goal they wish to achieve.
The client fails to keep focused or are easily distracted If the client isn't focused then they aren't present – and aren't benefiting from the session.	You can spot this through eye contact – but consider, for example: a) are you applying your own assumptions or perspective? b) are you making them feel uncomfortable, perhaps by sitting too close or giving too much eye contact?	• Check your observation and your criteria for making it. • This issue can't be ignored: the emphasis is on the coach to find out whether (and why) it's happening.
The client raises issues that may be best addressed with therapy or counselling	In intimate, confidential, one-to-one human interactions, people give you information about themselves, *and they are seldom inviting you to give them solutions.* So, it's vital that before you consider whether to address an issue with therapy or counselling, make sure that the client is offering it to you as an issue. Even if you're able and qualified to carry out such therapy or counselling, if your contract is for coaching the clients, it isn't appropriate to work in these other fields.	Be specific and clear to your client and yourself about what you are offering in a coaching session. If you do this, you will: • Be able to maintain composure (by being clear about your own purpose). • Help the client to map out their boundaries. • Successfully establish or maintain your own boundaries.

Difficult challenges for coaches	Issues to consider	Possible solutions
As a coach, you're having difficulty overcoming your own limiting beliefs An example of this is you coaching someone who is: older, younger, from a different culture, more educated, better paid or of the opposite sex.	A limiting belief stops you from giving your best. You need to be able to recognise these beliefs and manage your own responses to them.	The solution to overcoming a limiting belief is to use this test: <ul><li>Is this true?</li><li>All the time?</li><li>With everyone?</li><li>Everywhere?</li><li>Are there exceptions to this rule?</li></ul> Based on these answers, what would you like to believe? What is your aspiration?
The client seems to have one or more limiting beliefs	Are they willing to be confronted with this idea?	Consider whether you can contract with the client to find evidence that will help them change their view – for example, a client might agree 'if this happens six times then I will start to believe it/ not to believe it any more.' Remember, you can challenge the validity of a belief by asking the client how many times something had to happen before they believed it.
The client is angry or aggressive	View anger as a behaviour that you're observing and, crucially, manage your response. What is your response to anger? Is it the best one and could it improve? Next, focus on the client and move to resolve the issue with them.	Take several steps to respond to the issue for the client's benefit: <ul><li>Treat their anger as a response and a valid one.</li><li>Find out why the client feels this way.</li><li>Help them to achieve what they want.</li></ul>
As a coach, you feel stuck, uncertain, fixated or simply that you're running out of options	Self-awareness is vital for coaches – they shouldn't neglect their own situation. If you aren't self-aware, or if you haven't attended to your own development as a coach, then it's more likely that you'll find yourself either in a rut, uncertain or out of options. The first principle, therefore, is to stay aware and attend to your professional development.	<ul><li>Supervision for coaches – a different perspective can help produce a better approach.</li><li>Continuing professional development – for example, continuing to engage in development activities and mix with other coaches.</li><li>Reflect the dilemma back to the client – perhaps it mirrors how they feel, and it will be useful for them to know you're sharing their emotions.</li></ul>

Difficult challenges for coaches	Issues to consider	Possible solutions
Coaching when you're tired or exhausted	The issue here is that coaching requires you to be present for the *whole* session and this requires energy as well as physical and mental fitness. The client requires your undivided attention – your contract requires this as a minimum. As a coach, you also need to be finely tuned to the client's behaviour, and not just their words, and you need to focus on the client's issues so you can provide them with the best support. How well can you do this if you're tired? Also, coaching is a two-way process: clients can also be expected to observe their coaches (their physical and mental state).	Consider whether you're prepared for the client to comment on your physical condition or level of focus. For example: • How would you feel? • What would it mean for your credibility? • Do you know what it takes for you to be able to coach successfully? • How would you respond if the client commented on your lack of attention or tiredness? • Be aware of situations that take more energy from you than others, and plan your timetable for coaching accordingly.
As a coach you're concerned about maintaining integrity and independence when you have a commercial relationship	This issue relates to the two previous points about coaching: as a coach, you need to be absolutely clear about how coaching works and what it can achieve.	The solution is to be clear and transparent about coaching and your role as a coach, and to openly share this view in advance. From the outset, there should be an agreed contract between all stakeholders in the coaching relationship.
Experiencing what your client tells you they've experienced	One of the ways we make sense of what our clients tell us is by relating it to our personal experience. This empathy is valuable. However, coaches can sometimes become too empathetic because they can experience an issue too deeply, changing their state. At this point, they've lost perspective and are 'in the experience', unable to remain objective. This can also happen with positive issues, with the result that the coach fails to explore the issues or evidence sufficiently.	Good coaches understand that they can be supportive or sympathetic without necessarily empathising. An experienced coach understands that there is an optimal level of empathy, beyond which it is not helpful for the client. Remember, the client is not necessarily looking for a friend – they want a coach. It's unhelpful if coaches become as unresourceful as their clients because they've been over-empathising.

Difficult challenges for coaches	Issues to consider	Possible solutions
Managing conflicts of interest or working within the rules of engagement	One stakeholder in the coaching process is often the organisation, the client's employer. Your role is to enable the client to be more effective within the organisation – benefiting both the individual and their employer. So, there's no conflict of interest.	This requires coaches to be transparent in their purpose and should be clear from the beginning. Often, much is made (rightly) of the confidential aspects of coaching, but this relates to the *content* of each session. The *purpose* of the coaching has to be transparent if it's to work within an organisational contract.
The organisation's individuals insist on briefing you [the coach] about how to treat each client	This rarely happens, but if it does you need to explain that coaching isn't performance management, although it can assist in achieving the *aims* of performance management.	Be honest with the individuals about their expectations of coaching: their objectives and the best way to coach.
As a coach you experience immediate intimacy or attraction to your client due to the coaching relationship	This issue can sometimes occur in any coaching or therapeutic activity, where individuals confide with someone else quickly and deeply, sometimes sharing feelings that they may not have expressed with anyone else. This can lead the coach to feel that there's a level of intimacy and the key is that a coach can attribute intimacy to the wrong reasons.	The solution for the coach is to keep in mind the nature of the coaching relationship – people will share information based on their contract and professional relationship with the coach *and not for any other reason.*
As a coach you struggle to know whether, when and how to give clients the answers they need	If you're struggling with this issue, then you need to reposition yourself and go back to first principles – are you there to solve your client's problems, or are you there to help them find their own solutions?	Consider the **GROW** model – how close to achieving their outcome is the client on a scale of 1 to 10? Remind yourself of your purpose as a coach. Reflect your experience of this feeling back to your client – you've probably picked up their own feelings of frustration.

Difficult challenges for coaches	Issues to consider	Possible solutions
How should coaches respond to the clients who ask 'Just tell me what to do'?	Clients can forget (or not know) what coaching is about – they put you in the role of consultant or adviser. Alternatively, they have a relationship with you and trust your experience and breadth of knowledge. So they're prepared for you to tell them what to do. Imparting a relevant piece of information, or an example of what has been done by someone else in a similar situation, is perfectly acceptable as part of the coaching conversation – as long as you offer it as an option or for interest, rather than position it as advice.	Ask yourself which role you're in at a particular time: • Are you a consultant? • Your client's boss? • A mentor? • ...or a coach? Remind yourself of your purpose as a coach. You're there to help client find their own solutions, not necessarily to offer your remedy. Discuss and redefine the nature of the *coaching* relationship, and be prepared to discuss with them who they might go to for other kinds of help, if that's what they decide they might need.

PART FOUR

COACHING ISSUES AND PRIORITIES

Coaching is a highly dynamic activity and it is entirely in keeping with the nature of coaching that it should continually develop and evolve. In our experience, several perennial issues have assumed particular significance in recent years, not only for coaches but also for coachees and their organisations, and these deserve special focus.

- Team coaching
- Coaching supervision
- Cross-cultural coaching
- Mastery in coaching: the professionalism of the field
- Neuroscience in coaching
- Coaching for stress/pressure
- Insights from psychodynamic psychotherapy

TEAM COACHING

Team coaching is now a commonly used term, and many coaches who have built up their practice coaching one-to-one are being asked by clients to 'please come in and work with our team'. A frequent response to this request that coaches report back to us is 'what should I be doing if I'm contracted to work as a team coach?'.

OVERVIEW

We would recommend that anyone wanting to develop their skills and practice in the coaching field should build up their awareness of team coaching. This involves several different attributes, including the ability to:

- **understand how team coaching works;**
- **build an understanding of how high performing teams work;**
- **develop trust so that the team can agree a common vision and set of goals.**

In 2010, the Henley Centre for Coaching at Henley Business School ran a new open enrolment course on team coaching. It was well attended and the mix of individuals on the programme prompted some serious reflection about the subject once the three days was over. Some of the participants were freelance coaches who wanted to be able to offer team coaching as part of their portfolio to potential clients. Some of the participants managed existing teams in an organisation and wanted to improve team performance. Others were setting up new teams and wanted to get them off to the best possible start. The programme was almost a metaphor for the topic of team coaching itself: it needs a very clear and specific definition in order to be effective.

Research by Wageman et al (2008), quoted in *Leadership Team Coaching* by Peter Hawkins (2011)[1], states that in their research across 120 leadership teams 'very few teams were able to decode their successes and failures and learn from them without intervention from a leader or another team coach'. Another quote from the same source states: 'A surprising finding from our research is that teams do not improve markedly even if all

---

1 Hawkins, Peter. *Leadership Team Coaching*. Kogan Page, 2011.

their members receive individual coaching to develop their personal capabilities. Individual coaching can indeed help executives become better leaders in their own right, but the team does not necessarily improve. Team development is not an additive function of individuals becoming more effective team players, but rather an entirely different capability.'

Understand the continuum of team coaching

Hawkins describes a continuum of team coaching, which moves from team facilitation, through team performance coaching, to leadership team coaching and, finally, what he calls 'systemic team coaching'. This final stage picks up the idea that more traditional team coaching focuses too much on the internal aspects of the team, and too little on its external performance. This includes occasions when the team members are not together but are interacting with the critical stakeholders of the organisation in as broad a sense as possible. This considers the team to be a collective with a purpose, performance and process, with the personal and interpersonal development within the team to be a secondary issue. This is a long way from a simple interpretation of team coaching as a way of helping team members get on better together.

Use the right tools

Many of the tools and techniques in this book can be adapted and used with teams and members of teams. Useful examples include Force field analysis, MBTI, GROW and Visualisation and future orientation.

Read widely

A useful way of taking your understanding of team coaching further, and to identify areas you might want to practice, is by referring to a couple of excellent books on the subject. One is certainly *Group and Team Coaching: The Essential Guide*, by Christine Thornton[2], which offers a good overview of the theories of group dynamics, and how they apply to team coaching. The other would be the practical book already quoted on page 66, Peter Hawkins' *Leadership Team Coaching* (Kogan Page, 2010).

---

2 Thornton, Christine, *Group and Team Coaching: The Essential Guide*. Routledge. 2010.

Recognise the characteristics of high performance

Common purpose
Our vision
Our strategy

Complimentary skills &
competencies

Performance goals

Our shared approach
What we need from
each other
Personal safety & trust
& mutual
accountability

High
performance

Encourage team members to describe the qualities of a high performing team (what it means to them)

■ Individuals recognise their mutual dependence on each other.
They understand that this is the best way to achieve personal
and team success (people do not waste time trying to achieve
success at the expense of others).

■ Team members communicate honestly and openly. They take a
mature view of conflict, realising that it is unavoidable, trying to
work through the conflict as swiftly as possible and looking to
generate new ideas and understanding as a result.

■ Team members feel a sense of pride and ownership in the team
and are committed to the team's success. They also trust and
respect each other, providing encouragement and support,
sharing information and experience and communicating openly.

■ Individuals understand when the leader needs to act and make a
decision (i.e. in an emergency or if there is a major problem or
disagreement).

■ Team members are relaxed, determined and dynamic: they know
the team and understand their own strengths and weaknesses.

Focus on trust

Trust is about being able to clarify mistrust. At the limbic level, trust is knowing that 'I am safe'. The things we need to know in order to feel safe may vary between individuals. So, find out what it means for each individual. Safety can mean maintaining self-esteem, not losing face, or not being punished for things that are said or done.

Agree what the team wants

Encourage the team to answer these key questions.

1 What do we want as a team?
2 What stops us from getting it? What are the realities of our situation?
3 Based on these realities, what are our options? Are there any other possible options?
4 What action can we take right now? When will we take it? How committed are we?

Many coaching models, tools and techniques used with individuals can also be used with teams. To help you work with teams some useful interventions are discussed in Part 5 are.

- GROW
- Stress
- The Myers-Briggs Type Indicator (MBTI)
- Visualisation and future orientation
- Setting objectives and SMART goal
- ACS model (assess, challenge, support)
- Well-formed outcomes
- Heron's six categories of intervention
- Force field analysis
- Pareto analysis (problem solving)
- The decision-making process
- Decision-making principles and techniques
- Action-centred leadership

- Situational leadership
- Teamworking (Belbin's team types)
- 360-degree feedback
- Thinking strategically
- The balanced scorecard
- Developing innovation
- Six thinking hats

COACHING SUPERVISION

Supervision is an essential aspect of professional coaching, with the coach receiving practical support – for example, in separating their own issues from those being presented by the coachee.

OVERVIEW

At the time of writing, coaching remains an unregulated business. As well as moving towards more formal professionalism, receiving coaching supervision is becoming an essential element of a professional coach's practice. One of the main reasons for this is that purchasers of coaching (and endorsers of coaches) are making it an entry criterion for being considered for work as a coach. Organisations are increasingly requiring both external and internal coaches to be in coaching supervision before they will be considered to work with their managers. The various professional bodies of coaching all require individuals to demonstrate that they are actively receiving coaching supervision as part of their application for membership. Finally, any individual choosing a coach to work with in a private capacity would be advised by any friend or colleague with experience of the coaching field to make sure that the coach they choose is in supervision.

So, what is coaching supervision, and why is it so important? The original model comes from the kinds of supervision that practitioners in other regulated, 'helping professions' receive. It has long been the case that someone working as a counsellor, psychotherapist, social worker or clinical psychologist receives regular sessions of supervision, directly in proportion to the amount of client contact time they have. There are, of course, exceptions to this, but the regulatory guidelines of the official professional bodies in these fields make it clear that this is a requirement for acceptable professional practice.

Protecting the client and coach

Supervision is used for the protection of both clients and practitioners. The type of emotional stress and responsibility that results from working in close and intimate contact with other human beings, who are often in significant states of heightened emotion, can not only result in burnout of the 'helper', but also in the 'helper' being unable to continue to be effective with their client. The severity of the client's emotional state, and the nature of the presenting issues, may be less extreme in a coaching setting than it may be when visiting the professionals mentioned above (although most coaches will have experienced significant emotions in their coachees at times), but the impact on the coach can certainly be detrimental to their continuing effective performance.

Focusing on the client's issues

In order to coach others effectively, it is important for the coach to be able to separate out their own 'issues' from those being presented by the coachee. This is far more subtle and difficult than it might initially sound and requires a level of self awareness that is hard to achieve without an external perspective. A coaching supervisor is someone whose job is to listen and observe a coach talking about their experiences of coaching, and to help them understand when their own beliefs, values, preferences, judgements and personality are getting in the way of them being able to work exclusively on their client's issues. Without this external perspective, it is all too possible that, unknowingly, a coach can find themselves getting enmeshed in their coachee's issue, which has in fact triggered a personal response in the coach themselves.

The supervisor's responsibilities

The main responsibilities of a coaching supervisor are to provide:

- **knowledge and input;**
- **help for the coach to manage boundaries;**
- **support.**

The knowledge and input may include anything from insights into how the coach's behaviour with a coachee is affecting the work being done (perhaps from the supervisor's knowledge of psychodynamic principles, for example), to simple factual assistance, such as a useful book reference or suggestion for a coaching technique.

Boundary management is a topic which is frequently taken to supervision by coaches. These issues are often the ones which can otherwise keep a coach awake at night wondering if they have 'done the right thing' in a coaching session. The boundaries being examined can range from 'does this coachee need counselling or therapy instead of coaching?', to 'should I tell the coachee's boss that they have asked me to coach them on how to get a job with another organisation?', 'I'm finding myself personally attracted to my coachee, what should I do?', 'my coachee keeps asking me to talk about myself and I'm uncomfortable with doing this', 'the HR director of the company has asked me to report back to him on the content of the coaching sessions', and many other such concerns.

Support from a supervisor is important. Coaching can be a tough job and staying resourceful is vital for effective performance. Sometimes acknowledgement that you are doing your best is an essential intervention! If this can come from someone who knows your coaching world, and who you know has your best interests at heart, it can be very powerful and useful. As a rule of thumb, you should leave a coaching supervision session feeling better than you did when you went in to it. If you leave feeling reprimanded, criticised, patronised or in any other way 'less' than you were, find another supervisor.

The Seven-Eyed Supervision model

One model of supervision which is helpful in giving an understanding of the broadest context in which we need to think about supervision is the Seven-Eyed Supervision model. This was originally developed for those who supervise counsellors or psychotherapists but has now been used extensively in coaching supervision. The full description and explanation can be found in the seminal text on supervision, *Supervision in the Helping Professions*, by Peter Hawkins and Robin Shohet (Open University Press,

3rd ed, 2009). Here, we will present the basic concept to show the scope of the approach.

The model has seven 'modes', which direct the attention to different aspects of the supervisee's experience.

1 Focusing on the client and seeing *what* and *how* they present.
2 Exploring the strategies and interventions used by the supervisee.
3 Exploring the relationship between the client and the supervisee.
4 Focusing on the supervisee.
5 Focusing on the supervisory relationship.
6 The supervisor focusing on their own process.
7 Focusing on the wider context in which the work happens.

The diagram illustrates the relationships between these modes.

1. The client situation
2. The coach's inventions
3. The coaching relationship
4. The coach
5. The supervisory relationship and parallel process
6. The supervisor
7. The wider context

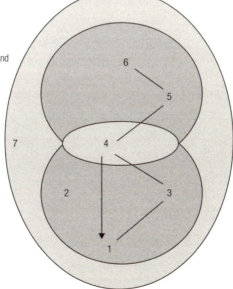

The Seven-Eyed model of Supervision
Source: Hawkins, P. (2009). *Supervision in the Helping Professions*, Open University Press.

Other useful models and techniques relevant to coaching supervision are discussed in Part 5.

■ **Coaching supervision**
■ **The meta-mirror**
■ **Parallel process, transference and projection**
■ **Cross-cultural awareness**
■ **Stakeholder analysis**

CROSS-CULTURAL COACHING

As people, organisations and entire economies become more connected than ever before, one of the great benefits and priorities of work is to connect with people from a culture other than your own. This is especially true with coaching. Coaching is never introduced into a vacuum but instead always takes place in the context of individual and cultural beliefs and behaviours; against this backdrop, a coach brings their own cultural and personal beliefs.

OVERVIEW

We would suggest that it is impossible to work in another country successfully without becoming aware and respectful of the history and customs of its people. The attitudes of the people we come into contact with are profoundly shaped by issues such as education, the historical events of their country, their politics and their religious beliefs (or absence thereof). However, when dealing with culture, it's important to maintain a balance between paying too much attention to it or not enough. Pioneers of cross-cultural studies have provided us with a wealth of frameworks and models. Seminal works by Edward T. Hall, Geert Hofstede and Fons Trompenaars formed the basis of subsequent studies and research and we would recommend any coach to read more on this important and fascinating subject.

What coaching universally deals with is enabling people to operate successfully and effectively, recognising each individual's different personal background and while always having to operate within their own culture. We recommend Dr. Jehad Al–Omari's book *Understanding the Arab Culture*

(How To Books, 2nd ed, 2008), which is an excellently balanced view of how much or how little emphasis should be given to cross-cultural issues. He describes managers who combine global vision with local imperatives as 'glocal' and we wonder whether there is a term for international coaches who coach locally and combine this with their international experience?

Jehad Al–Omari poses two questions about the role of culture and its impact on relationships.

1 What aspects of culture do you highlight or ignore and what is relevant and what is not?
2 From which angle do you start your analysis and how far in depth do you need to go?

These questions need to be asked of any cross-cultural coaching assignment.

The essence of cross-cultural coaching

'First do no harm' should always be the first rule of coaching. As we've said at various stages, coaches often arrive with credibility given to them by virtue of the fact that they have been engaged and supported by an employer. Coachees often, understandably, assume much, and attribute even more, to their coaches, giving them significant 'power'. The power to suggest through challenge, question and influence is one of the benefits of coaching, but one that needs to be given careful consideration. For instance, our most fundamental needs and how we satisfy them may vary from culture to culture. What a person needs in terms of being part of a group in the West may be very different to the way someone from the East satisfies their needs. The East tends to value *collectivism*, where deliberately trying to set yourself apart is not a valued approach. The West, on the other hand, is typically much more comfortable with individual success and account-ability. These different approaches have their advantages and drawbacks both on an individual and national level.

Coaches who work within different cultures need to be aware of their own fundamental needs and how they can impact their clients. Coaches who work as independents have often chosen to work independently and free themselves from organisations, and need to be self aware enough to know that this individual approach is not necessarily shared by those who are employing them.

The FIRO-B diagnostic instrument created by American psychologist Will Schutz identifies three main areas of human interpersonal need which are universal across cultures. This is explained in more detail in Part 5 of this book, but here we can look at how two of the concepts, affection and control (or competence), can be useful as reference points for our understanding of cross-cultural coaching.

Our fundamental needs as human beings include how much affection and acknowledgement we need from others as well as how much we wish to give in return, often displayed in the workplace and commented upon by our colleagues. Sometimes the imbalance between what we want and what we get causes us problems. How much we should give and receive can be dictated and imposed by societal norms and customs which we have to adjust to – sometimes easily, sometimes not.

Regardless of the type of society that we live in, or where we have come from, being good at something means we have a way of earning a living, and being included by our 'group'. Consequently, if we are able to become expert at something, we are more likely to be 'included' and able to exert greater control over our futures. It helps to be so competent at something that others need your expertise. It puts you in control. The West continually supplies 'experts' in a number of areas to emerging nations, people who are leaders in their fields and very competent in a particular area. In fact, being an expert is a great way of guaranteeing work.

Coaching definitions and ethics

We have had the unique experience of teaching the same model at Henley Business School in the UK within the British culture, attended both by local and international participants, and in more than 20 other countries – including the United Arab Emirates, Singapore, Malaysia and South Africa – where participants have been of the local population and share that culture.

Perhaps one of the greatest challenges for anyone who is teaching coaching is defining and explaining what it is, within a culture that has a clear idea of how information should be managed and how problems should be approached.

Professor Alison Hardingham, in her course notes for the Master of Science degree in Coaching and Behavioural Change at Henley Business School, explains that a coach is 'someone who helps another person or group of people articulate and achieve their goals, through conversation with them'. We go a little further and would add to this definition that coaching enables a person to become more effective.

Both definitions are broad, and most respectable programmes will spend time discussing and highlighting boundaries and boundary management. This is an important part of any coaching programme and is very necessary, because of the implications for individuals who can be influenced by a coach, someone who is given a large degree of authority.

We have spoken about the ethical dimensions and considerations of coaching in other chapters, in particular how they can be monitored and addressed by coaches in supervision. Clearly, the temptation to tell people what to do as a way of making them more effective is something that even experienced coaches must always guard against.

Certain cultures have successfully engaged in mentoring for centuries. Passing on knowledge from one generation to the next is often seen as important and even imperative. For example, the Chinese believe that to withhold one's experience and wisdom from those younger than you is foolishness. The question isn't why should you pass on your knowledge gained from experience, but why wouldn't you? Of course, the way in which people impart their wisdom to others can be affected by cultural rules and customs.

Respect is another one of those seemingly universal values with different behavioural descriptions dictated by culture. How respect is demonstrated in the UK differs from the way it is shown in China between the Chinese. In the UK, humour is highly regarded and is very much a way of life; people use it to chastise, offer different perspectives, challenge pomposity, lighten the atmosphere and avoid dealing with emotions. It is also used to share fun with others and communicate indirectly in many different ways. These differences are important and any coach with coachees from another culture needs to be aware of some of the most important aspects of that culture.

Without a clear methodology or familiarity with a coaching model, the way that many people and organisations help others to become more effective is simply to tell them what to do. In some cases this approach works, when we need to know what to do! At other times, even though we know what to do we simply can't do it. In this situation, we do not need to be told again; knowing what to do is not the issue here. This is the domain of the coach. Remember, coaching is about enabling, not teaching or telling: if you don't know how to use a computer, you need to go on a training course. If you don't think you're smart enough to use a computer, you need a coach.

Coaching is gaining popularity because it is *another way of enabling people to be more effective*. Crucially, it complements and does not replace other ways of achieving behavioural change, maintaining successful behaviours or enhancing performance.

Our experience of different cultures

Rather than list all the cultural aspects of any particular group that will affect coaching, we have highlighted below some of those that we experienced whilst tutoring on coaching programmes or coaching in one-to-one situations.

Our work in **Singapore** brought us into contact with coachees who were highly qualified, strong performers, very capable and indeed being fast-tracked for even more senior positions. In Singapore, the public sector successfully competes with the private sector for talent. Selecting candidates from the best universities worldwide, it has a preference for those with engineering degrees in line with the country's phenomenal growth and building programmes and its emphasis on maximising resources. Coaches have to be aware of highly intellectual approaches to many issues where time for reflection and personal development might be at odds with a results- and task-focused environment.

In this highly disciplined nation-state – where everything seems to work like clockwork and it seems that everyone is conscious of the rules – we were acutely aware of the need for our participants to understand the process of coaching. This includes the step-by-step approach to a coaching problem which could be solved with a coaching intervention and hence the belief held by many that the more 'techniques' one had available, the more successful the coaching session would be.

The advantages of being rule-bound are many but, as with most things, being too dependent on them can be challenging when rules no longer produce the desired effects. One of the challenges facing Singapore was a need to think creatively and to move away from the status quo which had worked so well for so long. Coaches needed to be able to stimulate their coachees by being challenging.

In the **United Arab Emirates (UAE),** many of the participants we met had been partly educated in countries such as the UK, USA, Australia, New Zealand and France before returning to work in their home country. The UAE has a population of around five million, of which approximately 20 per cent are nationals and the rest are expatriates from many other countries.

In a country where there has been a clear system of 'patronage', where the rulers and leaders endorse or decide what must be done, a culture exists where passing on the wishes of someone several times removed can have a lessened impact, and coaches in the UAE could face the challenge of understanding motivation in a coaching environment. Being told what to do does not necessarily provide motivation to do it. Whilst motivation is a universal quality that results in behaviour, the cultural rules within that society will affect our ability and tendency to reflect upon *why* and *how* we should do things. In this case, both the coaches and coachees have already bought into the higher level purpose of their leaders but may not be used to thinking about how and why they might need to do things more effectively.

We also found that many of the coaches in training had to deal with their own personal needs. This combined with a strong cultural bias towards passing on their experience in a helpful yet directive way that fitted comfortably with their cultural tendency to operate in this fashion and their familiarity with the system.

We were reminded of how different cultures are when one of our male participants mentioned the difficulty of coaching females. He said he would find it difficult to look at a woman for an hour. He wasn't referring to gender differences or being chauvinistic – he was simply referring to the cultural rules within his culture about the amount of time, the amount of eye contact and the level of conversation one could have as a male with a female within his culture. Clearly, for a Western coach whose culture prizes steady, non-wavering direct eye contact throughout a conversation, this would be a challenging concept.

In **Malaysia,** we found that warmth and friendliness exudes from people generally. Whether we met in business or not, Malaysians' hospitality and friendliness is palpable. Described as multiethnic and multicultural, the state religion of Malaysia is Islam. We were struck by the attitude of business leaders in this prosperous and industrious country, who held very generous views and opinions of their employees and colleagues and shared a sense of urgency to better society and pass on wisdom to the upcoming generation.

In one of our group coaching discussions, we met one leader who told us that his management style was guided by the five pillars of Islam. The five pillars are the tenets of the Muslim faith: 1. shahada (creed); 2. salat (daily prayers); 3. Ramadan (fasting); 4. Zakat (giving to the poor); 5. hajj (pilgrimage to Mecca).

In the UK, a country that prides itself on secularism, how would a coachee respond to a coach whose interventions were so intertwined with a religious belief system? Would it be possible for a coaching session to develop into a discussion about how to live one's life according to one's faith? How would one contract as a coach with a coachee if your religion is likely to inform your coaching? Is this still 'coaching'?

Coaches from other cultures will have numerous questions of fellow coaches in other countries and perhaps the easiest way to approach these questions is to identify how coaching is defined. This may sound easier than it is. In a mainly secular country like the UK where religion is optional, coaches spend little time establishing what drives a person's behaviour from this perspective whilst in many emerging nations, Islam and other religions are a way of life.

The role that race has played in **South Africa**'s history is undeniable and the country's current position compared to where it was only a few years ago is a testament to the collective efforts of its people. Racial awareness is more a way of life than it is in other countries with multi-cultural, multiethnic populations, purely by virtue of its relatively recent ascendancy.

Race was never an issue and we were never aware of anything except camaraderie and goodwill whilst working with our groups in South Africa. In fact, we were impressed and delighted by the application and perseverance of everyone who participated.

We were introduced to the participants of one group from the name sheet – prior to meeting any of them in person – by descriptions of their age, position and race. Our contact inferred nothing from the racial information, indeed spoke of each person with praise, but in giving us information about their race, it signified *something*. More importantly, it meant something to them.

When describing a coach or a coachee and adding their race to the description, what additional information are you giving and what are you receiving? We wondered what would be the difference between a coach who was Afrikaans, Indian, African or of mixed race? What information would a South African have about these coaches that someone from another culture would not? How would this information help or hinder them?

Understanding the significance of what is said

Paying attention to information is part of the art of coaching. When someone mentions something the question is not '*Why* is this significant?' but '*How* is this significant?'. Most people have either been on the receiving end or have heard the dismissive comment 'That's not relevant', perhaps from a teacher or trainer, but anyone who has asked the question will know that it was relevant because they asked it.

This skill is even more important in cross-cultural coaching than it is when working within one's own culture, where typically we have a much better idea of why things are mentioned and why they are important. Within our own cultures, we often generalise about people and situations: we have our own shorthand for shared concepts. In unfamiliar territory, we need to know the landscape, what the shared shorthand is and what that shorthand means to our coachee.

In Part 5 we offer a suggestion on how to approach cross-cultural coaching.

- **Cross-cultural relationships**
- **Mentoring**
- **GROW**

- Empowerment
- Situational leadership
- Neurological levels

ACHIEVING MASTERY IN COACHING

As coaching matures as a profession (or, in some people's views, matures towards becoming a profession), increased attention is being paid to how to define and quantify levels of proficiency. This is important for a range of stakeholders. For coaches, it is important that they can describe themselves effectively when developing business; for organisations, definitions matter when buying the services of external coaches as well as when they are developing internal coaching capability. For individuals, quantifying levels of proficiency matter if they employ the services of a coach for their own benefit and are faced with an overwhelming number of individuals to choose from. So, what is great professional coaching?

OVERVIEW

There has been much activity in the coaching world by various bodies and organisations setting out their stalls as 'professional bodies of coaching'. Significant progress is being made in terms of common terms of reference, codes of ethics and practice. However, at the time of writing, there is still no official 'professional body' appointed by an independent, appropriate authority. Indeed, in 2007, the prominent Australian psychologist and coaching expert, Anthony Grant, wrote: 'Because coaching is an industry, and not a profession, there are no barriers to entry, no regulation, no government-sanctioned accreditation or qualification process and no clear authority to be a coach; anyone can call themselves a 'Master Coach' (*The Handbook of Coaching Psychology, A Guide for Practitioners*, 2007). Much work has been done since 2007 by various coaching organisations and also by corporations developing their own criteria for recruiting coaches. However, the situation described by Professor Grant remains true today.

Despite this, the increased level of activity in the market around the 'professionalisation' of coaching means that for practising coaches, it is more important than ever to be able to articulate their own proficiency and have evidence to support their claims. This may be in the form of coaching qualifications (either academic Master's degrees or certificates from training companies), a track record of coaching clients and references, or membership of an appropriate coaching body.

Coaching clients, from individuals through to large corporate purchasers of coaching services, are now much more sophisticated, informed and aware of the criteria by which they decide whether to employ a coach or not. It is important, therefore, for a coach to have some way of assessing their own level of mastery, and then to be able to articulate it in a meaningful way to others.

We have offered some guidance in Part 2 around 'Articulating your coaching identity'. Into this, you might also want to include a reference to your own stage of 'mastery', and the evidence that you have used to make this judgement. You might find it helpful to refer to external frameworks of 'coaching competence', such as those produced by the International Coaching Federation (ICF), EMCC (European Mentoring and Coaching Council) or APECS (Association of Professional Executive Coaching and Supervision). The websites of these and other bodies will provide you with details of how they have articulated different levels of coaching capability. Some have very distinct graduations of level with competency frameworks and behavioural descriptors. Others have a specific set of requirements for membership, which imply a certain level of mastery, but don't make the distinction of a 'master coach'.

It is very much a personal decision for every coach as to whether they consider attainment of 'mastery' to be a linear process, with progress up through an externally specified series of 'grades', or a more holistic, personal development journey, based upon experience and reflection. Qualifications, and the source of the qualification (i.e. the awarding body for a degree, for example), can help your potential client feel more confident. Likewise, membership of one of the coaching bodies can be seen as indicating a certain level of status and competency. Mastery, in this sense, is very much in the eye of the beholder – these 'badges' of competence mean whatever the person or organisation on the receiving end makes of that type of 'quality assurance'.

We have certainly noticed that some purchasers of coaching services are still not that particularly well informed or sophisticated with regards to coaching, and are looking for the reassurance of the coaching equivalent of the now no longer used 'Corgi Gas Mark' (the UK industry regulation for safety standards in the gas supply industry). Unfortunately, the kind of official regulation which suppliers of gas appliances and workmanship are subjected to does not exist in the same official capacity for coaching. In this situation, attribution is everything – so being able to explain what 'Master Coach' means to a potential client is something worth thinking about. Whatever position you take on this, it might be useful to consider that the concept of 'Mastery' is very much 'out there' in the market place for coaching services, and it could be helpful to be able to explain yourself, professionally and intelligibly, in this context.

COACHING AND NEUROSCIENCE

Neuroscience is giving us insights into how the brain works and why we react to things such as change in the way that we do. This is a valuable and significant development in coaching.

OVERVIEW

It helps to think of people as having three brains, despite the fact that you may have got yourself into situations where you'd be hard pressed to believe you had one at all!

MRI scans during coaching sessions have shown the brain's activity whilst engaged in three of the main areas of coaching that a good coach will be trying to provide for a coachee: insight, relflection and motivation. When we have an 'Aha!' moment having reflected upon a situation and understood our reasons for not wanting to do something, and we accept that change is possible, our brain circuitry has changed.

Dr Paul Maclean, senior research scientist at the National Institute of Mental Health in the USA, refers to the 'Triune' brain, the three evolutionary brains that are the product of different stages in our evolution. All three brains are still present and have different functions.

The reptilian brain

This is the oldest brain responsible for basic functions such as the 'fight or flight' response as well as breathing, swallowing, heartbeat and visual tracking systems. Many animals have this in addition to humans and it is non-emotional. For instance, it is the part of the brain that a frog relies on to instantly catch and swallow an insect. The startle response is also governed here – an instant response for safety.

The limbic brain

As mammals separated from reptiles, they evolved in their reproductive process to carry their young *within.* This change in gestation meant that offspring were born defenceless and needed to be taken care of until they could fend for themselves. They needed the care of parents and other closely knit social groups in order to survive.

The limbic brain allows for verbal communication between a mammal and its offspring. Verbal cues are the way in which young mammals communicate their needs for food or attention. Lost or distressed youngsters will incessantly mew or howl until their parents return, while reptiles stay silent. Falling in love is a limbic response, as is the care we feel for our families and loved ones.

The neocortex

The newest brain is the intellectual brain. The neocortex allows us to reason. Human beings have the largest neocortex-to-brain ratio of any creature. This part of our brain allows us to engage in abstraction, to think of things in the future, to imagine and plan and to *reason.*

The domain of the neocortex is rational thought, persuasive, logical argument and lack of emotion. The neocortex doesn't feel – it thinks. When we have insights, we experience a limbic response.

The crucial question is this: when you coach, what do you think and how do you feel?

Most coaching sessions start with preliminaries and rapport-building. The first few minutes of a session are taken up with ice-breaking conversation that eases us into a place where we can begin to connect and get down to business. In second sessions, it's useful to use them to reconnect. During this period, the coach wonders what issues the coachee might find useful to discuss and explore in the session, whilst the coachee might be deciding on how and what they will present as an issue.

Very often, what is first discussed or presented is not what the session ends up being about. The maxim 'the presenting issue is never the issue' is an observation that refers to the consistent experience of professionals in a therapeutic setting. It means that, generally speaking, what seems to be the problem usually ends up being a symptom of it, rather than 'the' problem itself.

Coachees often present an intellectual issue, such as 'I'm struggling with meeting my deadlines this week' and those new to coaching often try to deal with the issue by using their intellect to help the coachee – such as some time-management skills input. When they do this, however, they are not coaching at all: they are consulting or mentoring. So, the next time you coach someone, listen to the issue or problem and then try asking 'Why is that a problem? or 'Why is that an issue?' and watch for limbic response – a non-intellectual answer from your coachee. The coach as a problem-solver is often not what the coachee needs. What he needs is someone who has observed that his perfectly reasonable, intellectual response seems to be at odds with his limbic response that encapsulates what he *feels*, rather than what he *thinks*.

An example of this struggle between what we know intellectually and how we feel, and how the emotions will hijack the intellect left to their own devices (simply because they happen faster – meaning that the limbic response is faster than the cerebral cortex) is illustrated by the following case study.

Case study: The neocortex vs. the limbic system

Stephen is partner in one of the 'Big Four' consultancies. He has been at partner level for several years and is in his early forties. He is married with two children, aged three and five respectively. His issue is his work–life balance.

He finds that he is going to work before the children wake up and returning from work after they have gone to sleep, thus seeing them only at weekends.

Intellectually, he knows that in his position, there will be sacrifices to be made. He was told this explicitly by more senior partners before his promotion. On one level, he knows that given his salary, the sacrifices are worth making. He sees many people around him in the same boat, and they seem to be managing.

On another level, Stephen is quite disturbed by the feelings he has when he thinks about his young children. He can't even cuddle them when he gets home for fear of disturbing their sleep, and he misses their hugs as much as they miss his touch. He gets quite upset if he thinks about it too much.

He reflects on his own childhood. Having been to a boarding school, he became used to separation from his parents during term-time and on an intellectual level, thinks he survived and is now doing well.

When faced with this issue, many well-meaning coaches will be feeling their own emotional responses to family and children kicking in and may have a strong compulsion to offer ways for the coachee to protect the family. In this and similar situations, managing your own response as a coach is something you must deal with *before* engaging with the coachee. Otherwise, your response could prompt them to subtly provide solutions that will fit with their reading of your response.

In this case:

1 observe the response of the coachee by noticing what they are feeling;
2 ask them how they feel about feeling that way;
3 ask them what they need to do about it.

At this point, the coach can begin the GROW model again quite effectively. Some useful models are featured in Part 5.

- **Neurological levels**
- **Questioning**
- **Visualisation and future orientation**
- **Miracle question**
- **GROW**

■ Wheel of life
■ Stress
■ Beliefs

COACHING AND STRESS

It is not common for coaches to be engaged specifically to help an individual deal with 'stress'. This is because admitting to being stressed leads other people to make all sorts of negative assumptions about someone's ability to cope, manage, lead and behave within an organisation.

OVERVIEW

Organisations may run stress management programmes for groups of employees, offering techniques and advice to enable them to maintain effectiveness whilst dealing with increased workload, responsibilities and ever-increasing uncertainty about the future. There is plenty of research into the link between workplace stress and the cost to organisations and the economy.

So, why, despite its significance and ubiquity, are people generally unwilling to talk about stress? The answer is because it's so difficult to define: it's hard to know if you're in danger of suffering from stress until you are. Admitting to it is also tantamount to admitting that you can't deal with the pressure of your job or your expectations of yourself. When you keep things to yourself, no one is able to help you.

The next challenge is to know when the pressure we are under is 'normal' or not. The law in the UK, for instance, is clear in its support for the premise that an employer is entitled to believe that an employee is up to the pressures attendant on a particular job. Furthermore, when it comes to whether or not we can do our jobs, 'The Court of Appeal also made clear that there are no special mechanisms within the law that apply to claims for psychiatric injury arising from doing the work an employee is required to do, and that the "threshold question" is whether or not this kind of harm to the employee was "reasonably foreseeable"'. (Sartain, Katsarou 2011, p.160[3])

---

3 Ibid.

With this in mind, it is not surprising that coachees can be reluctant to describe their attempts to cope with pressures as 'suffering from stress'. Nevertheless, how a coachee manages to cope with the external pressure of work and their own self-generated standards and expectations (no matter how unreasonable they are) is an area in which a coach often works.

Stress matters

How people deal with the pressure that leads to stress varies for each individual. Some people can become anxious at the thought of deadlines and anxiety levels build as they get closer, prompting them to make sure they have things ready by the deadline. Others feel no anxiety at all – for example, Douglas Adams, the English humourist and science fiction novelist, commented: 'I love deadlines. I like the whooshing sound they make as they fly by.'

Perhaps this reaction to deadlines might not be appreciated within organisations, but it would certainly be familiar to a lot of people and would definitely present an interesting and challenging issue for a coach.

How we deal with pressure and what we make of directives, management styles, comments or criticisms from our peers or line managers, the lack of encouragement or the amount of work we are given (or the way it is given) will vary. So too will our internal responses.

The difference between how individuals handle pressure and what constitutes pressure is huge and this has been highlighted recently by Denis Sartain and Maria Katsarou in their book *Under Pressure*, in which they give extreme examples of the way in which a number of individuals interpreted circumstances and reacted to them. For example:

In 2009, over a period of 24 months, 24 employees of France Telecom committed suicide, many of them blaming work as the reason they wanted to end their lives. On 9 September 2009, a technician in Troyes, southeast of Paris, stabbed himself in front of other staff after being told his job was to be cut. In August another employee, a 53-year-old father of three, killed himself in Brittany. 'Infantile management' and 'difficulties around high rank within the company' were blamed as reasons for his death. In the same month, a 28-year-old worker was found dead in his garage in a town in the east of France, having left a note that not only talked of his girlfriend but mentioned how 'helpless' and 'angry' he felt over the issues at work. In Marseilles, a 52-year-old employee killed himself on 14 July 2009, leaving a note in which he blamed 'overwork' and 'management by terror'. He wrote, 'I am committing suicide because of my work. That's the only reason'.

These extreme examples highlight how people can respond to the circumstances in which they find themselves. Other people within the same organisation may have received equally bad news or have perceived things in the same way, but they dealt with them differently. Perhaps they spoke to someone who was able to suggest alternative ways of dealing with their predicament, or perhaps they were able to simply talk about how they felt and doing so helped them to feel less hopeless.

Notice what's going on for your client

One of the main parts of a coach's job is to *notice* the coachee. This is done by calibrating or measuring their responses, such as *how* they say things and wondering why certain things they say produce changes in their physiology. These differences are often subtle but they are noticeable. This is especially significant if the change from one topic to another brings about a change in behaviour or outlook.

In fact, getting stressed involves going through a process. 'It is the process by which we allow external events and demands, as well as our own internal demands, fears, beliefs, to reach varying degrees of discomfort and ultimately, if not addressed, sickness. So, stress is an internal response to externally and internally generated stimuli.'[4]

Words and language, as well as physiological signs, are an externalisation or manifestation of what is going on for us internally. If we listen only to the content or the words alone, we can miss the physiological cues that can contain a great deal of other information.

Techniques follow later in this book but as so often is the case in coaching, being given the opportunity to discuss and reflect upon what

---

4   Ibid.

bothers us with a non-judgemental listener is one of the first and most significant benefits of coaching.

There are a number of references in Part 5 which might be useful.

- **Stress**
- **Wheel of life**
- **Reframing**
- **Work–life balance**
- **The meta-mirror**

INSIGHTS FROM PSYCHODYNAMIC PSYCHOTHERAPY

There are some fundamental ideas contained in psychodynamic psychotherapy (a type of psychotherapy where the therapist uses themselves and the relationship with the client as part of the work), which are important for coaches to know. They give us extremely valuable insight into some of the experiences which can impact strongly on our coaching relationships. The four main concepts are:

- **parallel process**
- **projection**
- **transference**
- **counter-transference**

OVERVIEW
Parallel process

This is the idea that as individual human beings, we tend to be 'ourselves' for most of the time. No matter how good we might think we are at playing roles, being on our 'best behaviour', or putting on a act for a particular situation or person, the real 'us' will shine through and be very visible to people on the receiving end of 'us'. So, the people we encounter have a pretty similar experience of the person we are, in reality.

This means that as a coach, if we take time to notice, and reflect upon, the impact our coachee is having on us, we are getting a great deal of very useful information which we might be able to use for the benefit of the coachee with their coaching issues. Even the impact of the first impression made by the coachee on us during our initial meeting or phone call, gives us information which might be hugely useful for our coachee, if they were aware of it. Very few of us have such excellent levels of self awareness that we are conscious of the impact we are having on other people in our daily lives. As a coach, simply feeding back to the coachee, at an appropriate moment, how you receive them, can create a real insight for them as to why they might be having a particular problem with other people. The basic principle is, if someone comes across to you, as the coach, as intimidating, then it is highly likely that this is how people in other relationships with them will experience them. If this behaviour is being done unconsciously by the coachee, then they are very likely to be unaware of why they get the responses they do from other people. And hence the issues they may well have brought to coaching for some help with…

Projection

If you have ever had the experience of being with another person for a while, and feeling emotions which, upon reflection, don't seem to 'belong' to you, you are on the receiving end of that other person's projected emotions. In other words, I can be feeling relaxed and pretty content with the world, with nothing particularly worrying me. A colleague comes into my office to talk about a meeting that's coming up that we have to go to, and even though there is nothing about this meeting which concerns me in any way, by the time he leaves, I am left in a state of agitation and anxiety. If I ask myself: 'Why am I feeling like this? Is there anything we just talked about that I hadn't thought of, and now I'm worried about something new?' and the answer to this kind of reflection is still 'No!', then I have 'caught' my colleague's anxiety and agitation.

Emotions are contagious! This is a biological truth for human beings, based on our fundamental evolutionary make-up. In our primitive days, no more than about 10,000 years ago, human beings were herd animals, living in groups and depending upon being in a group for their very survival. If a predator approached – another tribe, a hungry lion, (in our more sophis-ticated current times, an unpopular member of senior management…), then a 'fight or flight' emotional response would be communicated non-verbally, very rapidly amongst members of our tribe. This limbic level communication is still part of us today and, unless we are aware of it, we can fall in to the trap of 'post-rationalising' our emotional experience. In other words, in the example given at the beginning of this piece, after my colleague had gone, I might simply be left sitting in my office feeling anxious and agitated, and start rationalising these emotions in terms of why I *do* actually need to be worried about the upcoming meeting. Then I will adjust my behaviour accordingly, and probably be far less effective at the eventual meeting as a result.

Being aware of projection means that we can at least insert a 'pause' between experiencing an unexpected emotion and assuming that is a valid response relevant to us. As a coach, receiving projections of our coachees' emotions can give us another very useful source of information as to what is going on for them in their world at the moment. They might not be able, or willing, to tell us how upset or angry they are about something they are discussing with us. They might be talking about it in a very matter-of-fact way; very 'adult' and non-emotional. However, if, as we listen to them, we notice that we are beginning to feel upset or angry, for example, there is a fair chance that we are picking up their underlying emotion. This is then a significant additional insight in to how our coachee might actually be feeling and, at the appropriate time, we might be able to help them make real progress by asking them questions which allow them to get to this deeper level of understanding about their issue.

Transference

Transference is the process by which we attribute the features of one person we have (or have had) a relationship with, to another person or group of people. For example, let's say you had a very close relationship with your younger sister when you were growing up, and she had certain characteristics – she was small and lively, with blue eyes, curly brown hair and a Welsh accent. Then, when you are working as a coach in later life, and a new coachee walks into your office for a first session and she is small and lively with blue eyes and starts talking with a Welsh accent, it's quite likely that you will warm to her immediately, and attribute all kinds of things to her based upon your experience of your sister. You will, in effect, be transferring your totally valid responses to your sister onto a complete stranger! You might want to take a moment now to think about the 'types' of people that create a 'ah, you're one of those…' type of responses in you (if we're honest, most of us do this!). If 'one of those' turns up for coaching, as a coach we need to be able to notice our response, and manage it – it's our 'stuff' and we need to keep it out of the way so that we can create a new, clean relationship with the person who has just met us for the first time.

An understanding of transference is important to us as coaches from the other direction as well – our coachees may well experience transference for themselves when they meet us. If we remind our coachee, unconsciously or consciously, of someone else in their lives, they may well attribute features of that relationship, for good or bad, to their relationship with us. The most famous examples of this come from Sigmund Freud, the father of psychoanalysis, who gives us examples of his clients who were 'transferring' their feelings about their most significant early relationships, their fathers and mothers, to other, inappropriate relationships later in their adult life, with ensuing problems.

Counter-transference

This is the likely response evoked by transference if the individuals involved are not aware of the phenomenon. The transference occurs, as described above, emotions are projected and behaviours take place which then elicit responses from the recipient appropriate to the *original* relationship, but not to the one currently taking place.

For instance, a client comes in to the coach's office where they meet for the first time. The client has a strong resemblance to the coach's sister. Thinking of his sister makes him smile and feel good – and the client gets a really warm reception from the coach! (The coachee may deserve it in his or her own right, but the coach has hardly known the individual for long enough to respond that warmly just yet.) Getting that response however, causes the coachee to have certain emotions in return – maybe relief, warmth, relaxation, and so he or she behaves accordingly. They are now having a completely false relationship, based on assumptions that both are making about each other – and no doubt will get rather disappointed down the line when they finally do get to meet the 'real' coach and coachee.

This process, of course, can work with negative transference responses as well, where people respond cautiously, with hostility, suspicion or any number of negative emotions based on the feelings of past experiences.

As before, the main responsibility for coaches is simply to practise self awareness and to be alert to these kind of responses, both in ourselves and in our coachees.

A note of caution

Finally, we would reiterate that it is not appropriate for coaches to attempt psychotherapeutic interventions with their coachees. We say this categorically for several reasons:

- **psychotherapists spend many years in training, and in psychotherapy themselves, before they are ready to work with other people. Coaching training does not begin to approach this level of depth and intensity;**
- **even if someone is trained as a psychotherapist, they should not work in this space when they are working as a coach. The coaching contract is for a different type of work, the coachee has different expectations and the nature of a coaching relationship in terms of time available, duration of the relationship and frequency of sessions does not allow for psychotherapeutic work;**
- **issues may arise in a coaching session which the coach may identify as or suspect to be, ones which would better respond to psychotherapy. If this is the case, the intervention required is one of discussion with the coachee, and a suggestion or referral for this different type of work, if the coachee is open to it.**

PART FIVE

COACHING TOOLS, TECHNIQUES AND USEFUL MODELS

This section provides a range of practical tools and models to help coaches and benefit the clients they're coaching – the coachees. Some of these tools are universally relevant in a wide range of situations while others work best when addressing specific issues such as decisions and problem solving, leadership, relationships, prioritising, strategy and creativity.

The index at the beginning of this section lists all the tools and models referred to in the previous two sections, for ease of reference.

INDEX OF COACHING TOOLS AND TECHNIQUES

360-DEGREE FEEDBACK

Getting feedback from those around you is a valuable way of improving self-awareness, as well as being a powerful and revealing way to understand how you're viewed.

THE IDEA

When to use it: To help identify strengths, weaknesses and areas for improvement.

Summary: Coaching seeks to make people more effective and one of the ways we can become more effective is by knowing how our behaviour is being interpreted. 360-degree feedback is a process in which the people around you are able to make comments about your behaviour and what they would like to see you stop doing, do more of and continue to do. Coaches should always emphasise that feedback is based on observable behaviour – or the lack of it – within a specific context, and should never be taken for use as an indictment of the 'whole person'.

DESCRIPTION

There are many proprietary instruments for generating 360-degree feedback and it's useful for coaches to use the one that best suits them and their coachees.

There are several significant points to note about 360-degree feedback.

- **Feedback is a gift. Act on it or not, but it helps to view feedback in the spirit of a well-intentioned gift.**
- **360-degree feedback provides a valuable way of focusing on coachees' relationships and behaviour – those aspects that matter most to those around them.**
- **Feedback from a coachee's supervisor, employees or peers can be compared with a personal assessment (Myers-Briggs type indicator, for example) and self-reflection. A coachee can**

consider: what am I doing well? Where do I need to improve? How am I doing in relationship to my goals? What's important to me?

- It helps if coachees can shift their thinking from an understanding of their current behaviour to a broader and future-oriented vantage point.
- Most people who've experienced this type of feedback find that what some people want you to stop, others may want you to continue! This is a classic demonstration of how our behaviours are neither good nor bad, but are invariably context-dependent.
- 360-degree feedback prompts several fundamental questions. For example, if you want a result and you're not getting it, what behaviour or skill do you need to change or produce? Is this within your current range or do you need to develop this?

Coachees can sometimes confuse their lack of ability to behave in a certain way as an implied criticism of them as people. In short, they link their ability or lack of ability to do things with their self-worth. A coach should, therefore, take a person-centred approach, recognising that people are worthwhile and behaviours can be learnt, modified or deleted.

ACHIEVING A SENSE OF PURPOSE

Most of the time people in organisations are so task-focused that taking time for oneself is a luxury and it can become easy for us to forget our sense of purpose. Research and experience suggest that people have an innate need to make sense of their lives and the things they see around them. This simple reflective activity is designed to help coachees discover their sense of purpose.

THE IDEA

When to use it: To improve motivation or self-awareness or to help focus on career planning and achieving your long-term aspirations.

Summary: We constantly develop theories to explain why things happen as they do. Similarly, we have a need to attribute meaning and purpose to our lives – such as questioning how our day-to-day events contribute to the whole.

In answering such questions, we're defining and exploring our life's purpose and ensuring that our lives move in the direction we choose. Not everyone makes a conscious effort to develop and follow their life purpose – yet top performers do it consistently. It's this proactive, conscious approach that allows you to understand yourself, to set and achieve your long-term goals to gain control of your life and to be fulfilled.

DESCRIPTION

Understanding your sense of purpose

In this exercise, reflect on your life purpose by answering the following questions. (Your answers may take time to fully develop and will require complete honesty. Also, revisit these questions regularly, as your answers may change in the future.)

■ **What are my talents?**
■ **What am I passionate about?**
■ **What do I obsess/daydream about?**

- What do I wish I'd more time to put energy into?
- What needs doing that I'd like to put my talents to work on?
- What are the main areas in which I'd like to invest my talents?
- What environments or settings feel the most natural to me?
- In what work and life situations am I most comfortable expressing my talents?
- What do I want for myself?

ACTION-CENTRED LEADERSHIP

This classic leadership model provides a simple, practical guide for leaders who want to make changes and get things done.

THE IDEA

When to use it: When you're starting a leadership role or to help resolve a specific leadership challenge.

Summary: One of the most famous, enduring and useful views on leadership is John Adair's action-centred leadership model (see Adair, John, *The Action Centred Leader*, Spiro Press, 1988). Adair defines leadership in terms of three overlapping and interdependent circles: task, team and individual, and his approach emphasises these three areas as forming the boundaries for what the leader must do to be effective.

DESCRIPTION

Understanding action-centred leadership: task, team and individual

Adair's concept asserts that these three needs are central to the task of leadership. People expect their leaders to help them achieve the common *task*; build the synergy of the *team* and respond to *individuals'* needs.

- **The task needs work groups or organisations to come into effect because one person alone cannot accomplish it.**
- **The team needs constant promotion and group cohesiveness to ensure that it functions efficiently. The team functions on the 'united we stand, divided we fall' principle.**
- **The individual's needs are the physical ones (salary) and the psychological ones of recognition, sense of purpose and achievement and status, plus the need to give and receive from others in a work environment.**

For Adair, the needs of the task, team and individual overlap as follows:

■ **Achieving the task builds the team and satisfies the individuals.**
■ **If the team needs aren't met (the team lacks cohesiveness), then performance of the task is impaired and individual satisfaction is reduced.**
■ **If individual needs aren't met, the team will lack cohesiveness and performance of the task will be impaired.**

Adair's view is that leadership exists at three different levels: team leadership of teams of five to 20 people; operational leadership, where a number of team leaders report to one leader; and strategic leadership of a whole business or organisation, with overall accountability for all levels of leadership. At whatever level leadership is being exercised, Adair's model takes the view that task, team and individual needs must be constantly considered.

The strengths of the concept are that it's not culture or situation-dependent. Another strength is that it can help identify where the leader may be operating out of kilter with the real needs of the group or situation.

Leadership tasks

In order to fulfil the three aspects of leadership (task, team and individual) and achieve success, Adair argues that there are eight functions that must be performed and developed by the leader.

1 **Defining the task – the leader needs to ensure that the task is distilled into a clear objective that is SMART (specific, measurable, assignable, realistic and time-constrained).**
2 **Planning – this requires a search for alternatives, and is best done with others in an open-minded, positive and creative way. Contingencies should be planned for and plans should be tested.**
3 **Briefing – team briefing is a basic leadership function that's essential in order to create the right conditions, promote teamwork and motivate each individual.**

4 **Controlling** – leadership is frequently about getting maximum results with the minimum of resources. To achieve this, leaders need self-control, good control systems in place and to be able to delegate and monitor others effectively.

5 **Evaluating** – this function of leadership requires leaders to be good at assessing the consequences of actions, evaluating team performance, appraising and training individuals and judging people.

6 **Motivating** – a central task of the leader is to motivate others. The six main principles when doing this are: be motivated yourself, select people who are highly motivated, set realistic and challenging targets, remember that progress motivates, provide fair rewards and give recognition.

7 **Organising** – this function of leadership requires good leaders to organise themselves, their team and the organisation (including its structures and processes). Leading during times of change requires a clear purpose and an ability to organise effectively to achieve results.

8 **Setting an example** – leaders need to set an example to individuals and the team: a bad example is noticed more than a good one, and setting an example is something that must be worked at constantly.

These leadership functions need to be continuously developed and honed. In that way, leadership is itself a process of continuous development, education and improvement.

ASSESS, CHALLENGE AND SUPPORT

The ACS model (**a**ssessment, **c**hallenge, **s**upport) was created by the Center for Creative Leadership in North Carolina, based on its research into leadership development. The model is a useful and simple way of getting coachees to define their desired outcome.

THE IDEA

When to use it: When people need to identify or define their goals.

Summary: The ACS model provides coachees with a reflective process in which they can identify their objectives – what they want to achieve. This is accomplished with the three main areas of the model: assessment, challenge and support.

DESCRIPTION

The ACS model has three main elements.

Assessment

This is the stage at which the coach finds out about the coachees' reality and current situation; the coachees explain where they are in relation to where they want to be. As a coach, you gather data, beliefs and information, and find out what coachees do (or don't) pay attention to. Techniques such as 360-degree feedback are valuable for this stage.

Challenge

This is when a coach can begin to challenge the beliefs and stories in the coachees' information or data about their situation. The coach can also help the coachees develop self-awareness and challenge them, for example by checking statements or asking about commitment. Remember that challenges are most powerful when combined with support.

Support

This is about finding out what and who can best support the coachees. The coach offers support by a) finding out about options that are available and

b) encouraging the coachees to think about what support could be useful. The coach can offer information that can be supportive or which might result in support.

Support is vital if the coachees are to maintain their motivation, learn and grow. Support comes in many forms – for example, encouragement, empathy, active listening, learning, self-reflection, feedback or group sharing.

The ACS model, like the GROW model, isn't necessarily a linear process. However, managers who assess, challenge and then offer support are often viewed as people who know how to manage.

AVOIDING ACTIVE INERTIA AND MOVING FROM GOOD TO GREAT

Donald Sull, Harvard professor and author of *Revival of the Fittest*, believes managers get trapped by success, a condition he terms active inertia. Understanding how inertia arises is a large part of avoiding or resolving it.

THE IDEA

When to use it: To avoid complacency or when coachees need to develop or implement a new business strategy.

Summary: Active inertia occurs when managers respond to disruptive changes by repeating (and usually accelerating) activities that succeeded in the past. They actively work to stay rooted in the past, believing that an established (and in reality, outdated) formula will bring success. However, if circumstances have changed this can often mean that the firm is simply digging itself further into a hole. Several simple techniques can help avoid active inertia.

DESCRIPTION

Active inertia is overcome by changing or transforming a business's priorities and commitments. If active inertia grows as a result of the company's current priorities – its strategies, processes, resources, relationships and values – then changing these will make the company less likely to fall back on the status quo. However, transforming priorities and commitments isn't without risks: making them work depends on the company's financial security, competitors' likely responses and management's ability to lead the transformation.

How active inertia works

1 A firm correctly discerns gradual shifts and developments in the external environment, but then fails to respond effectively when they see these changes coming.

↓

2 Managers get trapped by success, often simply responding to the most disruptive changes by accelerating activities that succeeded in the past.

↓

3 The source of active inertia is a company's success formula, the unique set of strategic frames, resources, processes, relationships and values that collectively influence managers' actions.

↓

4 With time and repetition, people stop considering alternatives to their formula. The individual components of the success formula grow less flexible. Complacency grows and problems

To understand the extent to which your organisation is at risk from active inertia, consider two questions.

■ **Could external developments threaten your core business? How (in what way)? When (in what circumstances and how will you know)? Why will you be vulnerable?**
■ **Do you have an agreed, robust alternative to the status quo?**

Scenario thinking is a comprehensive technique that can help you avoid the perils of active inertia. There are a number of other measures to help avoid this situation.

■ **Recognising that revolutions fail, flywheels succeed. Jim Collins, author of the bestselling book *Good to Great*, argues that dramatic change programmes, revolutions and restructurings may save the day but they do little to sustain or develop success, or advance the business to greatness. In fact, there's no single action that can do this. Collins likens the process to relentlessly** pushing a heavy flywheel in one direction, steadily building up momentum until a breakthrough is achieved. No single push makes the breakthrough; rather, it's the cumulative effort that ensures success.

Collins' research reveals several interesting points. First, moving from good to great is a cumulative process: it happens step by step, action by action and leads to sustained results. Also, good-to-great companies had no name for their transformations. There was no launch event, no tag line, no programmatic change. There was no miracle moment. Finally, great companies artfully manage the process of changing, achieving commitment without having to emphasise it. Under the right conditions, the problems of commitment, alignment, motivation and resistance to change melt away. There really is no substitute for strong, capable leadership.

■ **Keep in close touch with external realities and confront the brutal facts.** In retrospect, people in failed organisations often blame changes in the marketplace that passed unnoticed at the time. Typical examples include new products and new substitutes coming on the market, changes in product technology, demography, income distribution, fashion and a cyclical fall in demand that wasn't taken seriously. Similarly, increased competition often went unnoticed, while in retrospect the signals were there to see (e.g. technological change lowering rivals' costs, a lack of strong product differentiation or strong cost advantage and low or falling switching costs for customers).

■ **Develop a culture of discipline and entrepreneurship.** All organisations have a culture, some have discipline, but only a few have a culture of discipline. This matters because, for example, disciplined people don't need hierarchy. Disciplined thought removes the need for bureaucracy, and discipline combined with entrepreneurship results leads to great performance.

■ **Use technology to accelerate changes.** Great companies never rely on technology as the primary way to develop their business,

but they're expert at applying carefully selected technologies. By itself, technology is never a primary cause of greatness or decline.

There's much that executives can do to prepare for genuine opportunities – or to weather a crisis. The secret to success lies not with heroic, high profile actions, but in the quiet actions taken during periods of relative calm and success.

THE BALANCED SCORECARD

The balanced scorecard approach generates objectives in four pivotal areas of business that will help achieve the strategy. The scorecard then provides a way to work on each of these vital areas, with progress being regularly assessed.

THE IDEA

When to use it: When coachees need to develop or implement a business strategy.

Summary: In their bestselling book *The Balanced Scorecard,* Robert Kaplan and David Norton explain how to increase the long-term value of the business. Their approach applies the concept of shareholder value analysis and is based on the premise that the traditional measures used by managers to see how well their organisations are performing, such as business ratios, productivity, unit costs, growth and profitability, are only a part of the picture. These measures are seen as providing a narrowly focused snapshot of how an organisation performed in the past, and give little indication of likely future performance. In contrast, the balanced scorecard offers a measurement and management system that links strategic objectives to comprehensive performance indicators.

DESCRIPTION

The success of the balanced scorecard approach lies in its ability to unify and integrate a set of indicators which measure the performance of key activities and processes at the core of the organisation's operations. This is seen as being valuable because it presents a balanced picture of overall performance and highlights specific activities that need to be completed. Furthermore, the balanced scorecard takes into account four essential issues of which traditional 'hard' financial measures are only one part. The three 'soft', quantifiable operational measures include:

- customer perspective – how an organisation is perceived by its customers;
- internal perspective – those issues in which the organisation must excel;
- innovation and learning perspective – those areas where an organisation must continue to improve and add value.

The type, size and structure of an organisation will determine the detail of the implementation process; however, the main stages involved include:

1 **defining the strategy** and ensuring that people have an understanding of the strategic objectives and the three or four critical success factors that are fundamental to achieving each major objective or goal;

2 **deciding what to measure.** Goals and measures should be determined for each of the four perspectives (finance, customers, internal processes and innovation and learning);

3 **finalising and implementing the plan.** Invariably, further discussions are necessary to agree the detail of the goals and activities to be measured, and what precise measures should be used. Each measure needs an action to make it happen, and this is where the real value in the approach lies: deciding what action to take to achieve the goal;

4 **using the results.** While everyone should understand the overall objectives, deciding who should receive specific information, why and how often, is also important. Information needs to be used to guide decisions, strengthening areas that need further action. Evidence suggests that being seen to act can be as important as the action itself;

5 **reviewing and revising the system.** As with any management process, a final stage of review and revision ensures that lessons are learnt and any new challenges are set.

BALANCING WORK AND PERSONAL LIFE

Becoming successful in life and in your career requires alignment between three vital parts of your personality: your principles, goals and behaviour. Coaches will benefit as much from this technique as their coachees.

THE IDEA

When to use it: To reduce stress and improve personal effectiveness – for example, when starting a new role.

Summary: Living in balance or alignment means achieving equilibrium between your personal and professional life. The two are closely linked and if you neglect either then this results in an increase in stress and a decline in motivation and performance. However, finding the right balance is an entirely personal matter influenced by such variables as an individual's situation and personality.

DESCRIPTION
Living in alignment

Living in alignment can be seen as the interconnection of three frames:

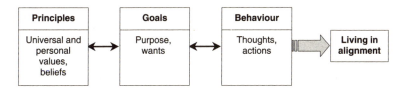

The first box contains your *principles*, personal values and beliefs. The second frame holds your *goals* – ranging from your life purpose to things you'd like to have or achieve. The third frame contains your *behaviour*, including inward thoughts and outward actions. Living in alignment simply means that your behaviour is consistent with your goals and that your goals are consistent with your principles and values.

Achieving alignment (and greater balances and satisfaction) depends on each individual's specific principles, goals and behaviour. Also, it's not only the range of issues that cause misalignment but the type of people experiencing it and how they react. The solutions are personal, but they typically include some of the following actions:

■ **set your own priorities – and then stick to them;**
■ **keep your commitments – this can mean living your personal life as you would your professional life; keeping the same standards of behaviour;**
■ **know yourself – understand what causes you stress, when you're likely to become stressed, and how you can avoid these situations;**
■ **take responsibility – too often people either deny their situation, which often makes things worse, or blame someone (or something) else. Even if it's the fault of someone else, it's you that's being affected and you who needs to resolve it;**
■ **consider what's causing stress – acknowledging the existence of stress is only the start: the next step is to identify the source of the stress. Rationally consider how to overcome the causes. This can take time, as stress is rarely removed in one leap but often requires action in a range of areas;**
■ **anticipate and plan for stressful periods (at work or at home) – this may include getting temporary resources or people with specific skills to help;**
■ **develop strategies for handling stress – consider what may have worked for you in the past. Also consider removing or reducing the cause of stress, or learning to accept it if it can't be removed;**
■ **relax – this is easier said than done, but the key is to understand that you need to work at relaxing!**

CAREER DEVELOPMENT PLANNING

Personal development and career planning needs careful consideration and it may help coachees if they create a personal profile highlighting relevant skills, experience, strengths and weaknesses. These can be matched with aspirations and likely challenges – both now and in the future.

THE IDEA

When to use it: To turbo-charge your career and help plan for future progression and success.

Summary: Personal development and career planning enables people to move from where they are to where they want to be. It's a lifelong process of nurturing, shaping and improving skills, knowledge and expertise, in order to enhance effectiveness and adaptability. Personal development and career planning also reduces the likelihood that skills will become out of date or obsolete.

It doesn't necessarily mean preparing for promotion or advancement, although that might be relevant from time to time. It's much more about improving and being ready for new challenges and changing circumstances. Development planning requires a personal commitment to develop and improve. In particular, this means understanding and accepting constructive criticism and being willing to take measures to improve performance.

DESCRIPTION
Develop your personal profile

This can be created by considering the following factors.

- **Priorities. What values really matter to you personally? Do you know what sort of leader you want to be? It can also help to reflect back over your career and recollect leaders that you feel** were particularly good or especially poor. Why did they succeed or fail?

- **Work experience.** What positions have you held? When did you succeed and why? How could your performance have been better?
- **Achievements**. What have been your greatest achievements? What gave you greatest pleasure and what impressed others?
- **Personal attitudes.** Assessing how you behave in different situations can help to understand the way you feel and behave – where you are likely to be strong and when you might feel less certain. There are a number of questions you might ask yourself.
  - Are you energised around people or do you prefer to spend time alone?
  - Do you think quickly or do you need time to reflect before speaking?
  - Do you prefer to do a few things well or pursue many things superficially?
  - Are you an open person or more private?
  - Do you prefer order and structure or do you tend to live spontaneously, remaining open to possibilities?

Assess your future options and plans

The value of a personal profile lies in helping you to understand yourself: what you like and dislike; where you succeed and fail, and when you're strong and weak. It's a valuable tool when starting to think about self-development, or when assessing your achievements, preferences, skills, strengths and weaknesses.

There are several key questions that can help support an individual's career planning and development.

- **What are your goals and aspirations? Why are these important?**
- **What is your timescale for achieving these goals, and what are the key milestones that will need to be achieved?**
- **Are your development plans in line with the goals you want to pursue?**
- **What opportunities are available – now and in the foreseeable future?**
- **How do your skills match with the business strategy?**

- What further support do you need?
- How will you ensure success?

Follow the self-development cycle

The self-development cycle is a method of planning development activities in a rigorous, thorough and practical way. Its success depends on repeating the planning process regularly (at least every year; preferably every six months or when circumstances change, such as when you take on a new role).

There are seven stages of the cycle.

1 **Establish the purpose.** You need to keep the overall aim firmly in mind and then ensure that all activities directly support this aim. Without this clear goal, it's often difficult to stay on track, keep momentum or maintain motivation.

2 **Identify development needs** so that a programme for meeting those needs can be devised. In particular, the needs must be realistic and time-constrained, with a definite deadline.

3 **Look at your opportunities for development.** Deciding how to meet the development needs is the next stage and this may include a mix of formal and informal methods. As well as effectiveness, cost and timing, think about your own preferred learning style: what approach suits you best?

4 **Formulate an action plan.** This will be necessary for more complex development needs requiring a range of activities or an ongoing process. You should also consider how the development process will be supported, perhaps by a mentor.

5 **Undertake development.** This is the core of the process. It's worth considering specifically how the results will be integrated into workplace activities.

6 **Record outcomes.** Keep track of development activities in order to assess results against planned objectives – review progress and understand what methods work best – and plan future activities.

7 **Review and evaluate.** Evaluating an event will help to assess whether the original objective has been met and the development needs fulfilled.

CIRCLES OF EXCELLENCE

The circle of excellence works well when a coachee has the ability but lacks the confidence to succeed, usually in a new situation.

THE IDEA

When to use it: When a coachee lacks confidence but, crucially, possesses the skills needed to succeed.

Summary: One way to help people summon up their confidence is a technique called the circle of excellence. Crucially, it doesn't develop competence in a skill but instead assumes ability. This technique teaches coachees to plan for the future using the best of their past or the past of someone they know. In other words, to access skills and states of mind which have worked well in previous situations, and transfer them to the problem situation. It enables coachees to access their best state of mind any time it's needed.

DESCRIPTION

The circle of excellence includes several steps that need to be practised in advance so they can be drawn upon at will.

1 Imagine an invisible circle on the floor, large enough for you to walk into (e.g. about three feet in diameter and about two feet in front of you).
2 Step inside the circle and imagine a time when you were brilliant at what you want to be doing. Imagine that everything went well and you were bright, happy, confident, full of energy and very successful at your task. Think of all the feelings you experienced – how you succeeded and how it made you feel. If you don't have this particular personal history, *just pretend that you do*. In your mind, visualise and step into the shoes of someone you admire who would achieve this goal.

Interestingly, our brains cannot tell the difference between a *real* history or an *imagined* history, or even the history of others, so all you have to do is emotionally capture that feeling of excellence using whatever role models or scenario-playing works for you.

3 Develop a full visual, auditory, kinaesthetic representation of the way you feel. Use all your senses to actually *feel* what it's like. See yourself in the circle being wonderful. Visualise it fully. Hear and feel what's going on around you.

4 When you have sufficient detail in your mind, step into the picture of yourself, imagine it's as if you step into that person and that experience.

5 Finally, get comfortable with these feelings so you feel able to draw upon them at will. This may mean practising the situation or finding a specific phrase or mental or physical cue so you can recall those feelings when needed. That might be tapping your fingers, holding your arms in a certain way or whatever physical link you can easily and accurately repeat.

If you feel stressed in the future, you can trigger the physical link and the feelings that you've experienced will return as soon as you're back in your circle of excellence.

COACHING SUPERVISION

Professional supervision enables coaches to reflect on their work, either with a professional coaching supervisor, in a facilitated group or with their peers. The primary purpose of this reflection is to better understand challenging and complex situations and to increase clarity and effectiveness. Supervision is also an opportunity to receive practical and emotional support, and is a valuable way of learning and developing coaching skills.

THE IDEA

When to use it: Whenever you're in a formal coaching relationship.

Summary: Supervision has been practised in social work, psychotherapy, counselling and clinical psychology for many years. It provides a range of benefits and requires a clear, simple but disciplined approach with several basic techniques.

DESCRIPTION
The benefits of supervision

Supervision benefits coaches and their clients. Management by the supervisor ensures that the coaches are working responsibly and to the best of their ability, and also ensures an informed check on quality and ethics. Supervision provides coaches and their organisations with several important benefits.

- **Educational development of coaches and the fulfilment of their potential. The goal of supervision is to remove misunderstandings or misconceptions and improve coaches' skills. This is achieved by encouraging coaches to reflect on their work.**
- **Practical and psychological support. The stresses and pressures of coaching can affect work performance and take their toll psychologically and physically. The supervisor's role is to help coaches manage that stress more effectively and provide reassurance and emotional support.**

- **Quality assurance.** Supervision promotes consistent standards and best practice. The supervisor promotes the norms, values and best practices of being a coach. Monitoring professional and ethical boundaries is also part of the coaching supervisor's role.

The supervisor's role and responsibilities

- The supervisor shares with coaches all responsibility for ensuring that their coaching work is professional, ethical and as successful as possible.
- The supervisor provides feedback or direction that will enable the coaches to develop the skills, theoretical knowledge and personal attributes needed to succeed as a coach.
- The supervisor listens, supporting and challenging the coaches whenever personal issues, questions, concerns or insecurities arise.

Format and guidelines for supervision

- Supervision often involves a presentation of a specific case or a set of issues that are concerning the coach.
- Supervision occurs in either one-to-one or group sessions.
- Coaching consultancies typically recommend a ratio of supervision to coaching hours. This varies depending on the amount of coaching a coach is doing at any one point. One hour of supervision to 12 hours of coaching is a common guideline.

Supervision is about coaching and supporting and the coach. When this happens well, everyone involved in the coaching arrangement benefits.

DECISION-MAKING PRINCIPLES AND TECHNIQUES

Coachees will find two issues invaluable when making decisions: they need to understand the psychological aspects and pitfalls and also know how to apply the right techniques at the right time.

THE IDEA

When to use it: When problems need to be solved or any decision is needed.

Summary: Decision making is deceptive: it can seem straightforward to understand the essentials of a problem or situation and then decide what to do next. However, reality is seldom that simple. Decisions require a range of skills and techniques, as well an ability to avoid potential pitfalls.

DESCRIPTION
Avoiding mistakes when making decisions

The way that people think, both as individuals and collectively, affects the decisions that they make, in ways that are far from obvious and rarely understood. John Hammond, Ralph Keeney and Howard Raiffa recognised the following traps in decision making (see their article *The Hidden Traps in Decision making*, Harvard Business Review, September-October, 1998).

Potential pitfalls for decision-makers...	...and how to avoid problems
The *anchoring trap* is where disproportionate weight is given to the first piece of information that we receive. The initial impact of the first piece of information, our immediate reaction to it, is so significant that it outweighs everything else, 'drowning' our ability to evaluate a situation.	• Be sure about what's happening. • Wait as long as possible to ensure that you have all the information. • Always look for different options. Key question: Are you giving undue influence to a piece of information?

Potential pitfalls for decision-makers...	...and how to avoid problems
The *status quo trap* biases us towards maintaining the current situation – even when better alternatives exist – either because of inertia or because of the potential loss of face if the current position were to change.	• Value openness, honesty and courage. • Build a positive, blame-free culture. • Instil a questioning approach. • Encourage diversity, experimentation and learning. Key question: Is your decision or approach influenced by a simple reluctance to change?
The *sunk-cost trap* inclines us to perpetuate the mistakes of the past, because the investment involved makes abandonment of previous decisions unthinkable. This situation is also known as an escalation of commitment, a flawed way of coping with – rather than simply making – decisions.	• Adopt the management accountant's view: if it's spent, it's spent – worry about the present and future, not the past. • Be aware that this flaw is particularly significant when it comes to managing risk and investing in new projects or deals, such as acquisitions or capital investments. • Plan carefully and know in advance where the plan can be modified and by how much. • Maintain a clear focus on the desired outcome and keep an overview of the whole situation. Key question: Are you using your decision to protect past investments?
The *confirming evidence trap* (confirmation bias) is when we seek information to support an existing view or preference and discount contrary information, to justify decisions and to support the continuation of the current favoured approach.	• Challenge and test existing assumptions as a way of identifying weaknesses in your thinking. • Research alternative approaches and ideas. Key question: Are you filtering information to suit a particular belief or preference?
The *overconfidence trap* makes us overestimate the accuracy of our forecasts. Linked to confirming evidence, it occurs when decision-makers have an exaggerated belief in their ability to understand situations and predict the future.	• Reduce or remove the factors causing overconfidence e.g. a lack of sensitivity, excessive routine, a lack of criticism, feedback or review. • Research, investigate and understand all of the possible options. • Act appropriately by avoiding quick or hasty decisions. Key questions: Do you feel you have complete mastery of the issue – and could this confidence be misplaced?
The *framing trap* is when a problem or situation is incorrectly stated, undermining the decision. This is often unintentional, but not always. How an issue or situation is seen is important in providing the basis for developing an effective strategy or decision. The framing trap often occurs because well-rehearsed and familiar ways of making decisions tend to be dominant and difficult to change. This trap may lead managers to solve the wrong problem – decisions may have been reached with little thought and better options may be overlooked.	• Recognise that managers habitually follow established success formulas and, as a result, view new issues through a single frame of reference. • Understand that people's roles and situation within the organisation influence the way problems are framed. • Make sure you have accurately defined the problem. The framing trap can occur because of poor or insufficient information; a lack of analysis; a feeling that the truth needs to be concealed, possibly out of concern; a desire to show expertise, or a belief that they have to handle it, and a lack of time to correctly frame the problem. Key question: Would reframing broaden your thinking, improving the decision or the way it's implemented?

Potential pitfalls for decision-makers...	...and how to avoid problems
The *recent event trap* leads us to give undue weight to a recent, possibly dramatic, event or sequence of events. It's similar to the anchoring trap, except that it can arise at any time – not just at the start – and cause misjudgement.	This is similar to the anchoring trap and, as before, awareness of this trap and the dangers it might pose are vital for avoiding it. Key questions: Are you maintaining a sense of perspective? Do you have the most recent event in context – what's the story up to this point?
The *prudence trap* leads us to be overcautious when estimating uncertain factors. There's a tendency to be very risk averse and this is likely to occur when there's a decision dilemma – when the decision-maker feels both the current approach and alternative courses carry risks.	• Set the parameters for risk and show where the boundaries lie. • Encourage a blame-free environment, where experimentation is allowed, properly managed and controlled. • Remember that it's a flaw to be overcautious. Realism, perhaps erring on the side of caution (depending on the nature of the decision), is the antidote. Key questions: Are you being too cautious? Do you have the right balance between risk and return?

As well as these thinking flaws and coping patterns, there are two other pitfalls resulting from the culture of an organisation: *fragmentation* and *groupthink*.

Fragmentation occurs when people are in disagreement, either with their peers or their superiors. Usually, the expression of emerging dissent is disguised or suppressed, although it may appear as 'passive aggression.' Dissenting opinion often festers in the background – mentioned informally in conversation, rather than clearly raised in formal situations, such as meetings. Fragmentation is corrosive, hindering effective analysis and decision making, and can worsen when the views of one group dominate. It also feeds off itself in a self-sustaining cycle, as any move to break it is seen as an attempt to gain dominance by one side. It can, therefore, become locked-in to the organisation and be extremely difficult to reverse.

Groupthink is the opposite of fragmentation. It occurs when the group suppresses ideas that are critical or not in support of the direction in which the group is moving. The group appears to be in agreement or certain but is neither. It's caused by many factors, such as past success breeding the belief of an infallible team and complacency. Groupthink may occur because the group is denied information or lacks the confidence or ability to challenge the dominant views of the group. People may be concerned about disagreeing, either because of past events, present concerns or a fear of what the future might hold; they therefore seek safety in numbers.

Groupthink is exacerbated by the fact that cohesive groups tend to rationalise the invulnerability of their decision or strategy, and this in turn inhibits critical analysis and the expression of dissenting ideas. The effect is an incomplete survey of available options and a failure to examine the risks of preferred decisions.

Groupthink can occur in organisations where teamwork is either strong or weak. As with fragmentation, groupthink is self-sustaining. The longer it lasts, the more entrenched and 'normal' it becomes. It can be very difficult to reverse.

Principles and techniques when making decisions

- **Be bold and don't fear the consequences of decisions** – we tend to overestimate the consequences, good and bad, of our choices. We also tend to discount our ability to make the right choice. This results from 'loss aversion': the view that a loss will hurt more than a gain will please. Remember, the worst-case scenario might never occur and even if it does, people invariably have the psychological resilience to cope.
- **Trust your instincts and emotions** – sometimes, quick decisions work best precisely because you've picked up on the key pieces of information quickly and then responded. More time can simply lead to information-overload and new distractions.
- **Play devil's advocate** – searching for flaws and failings will strengthen your decisions and illuminate factors affecting the decision and other issues, such as biases. This means being aware of confirmation bias and using it.
- **Avoid irrelevancies** – irrelevant information distorts our perception, as described in the anchoring trap. The solution is to be ready to question the context of the information. What are you basing your decision on, and is it really relevant?
- **Reframe the decision** – this will help you view the issues from a new perspective.

- **Don't let the past hold you back** – the sunk-cost trap highlights our tendency to stick with previous choices because too much has been invested. Don't! Better alternatives may exist.
- **Challenge groupthink** – people are often afraid to comment or to act because of social pressure. This is a poor excuse. Find out what people really think and use that to inform decisions.
- **Limit your options** – this is the paradox of choice: the more options we have, the harder life can be. Choose the most promising options; this can help to remove pressure and clarify your thinking. We're fixated with choices, believing more to be better. In truth, less choice can be more satisfying. Also, it may be worth delegating the decision to someone else better qualified.

THE DECISION-MAKING PROCESS

Decision making is central to business success and generating new ideas – so it's a likely issue for your coachees – yet it's littered with hazards. Understanding the pitfalls is important; so, too, are balancing rationality with intuition and trusting yourself. It's often helpful for individuals to keep in mind a clear process or structure when making decisions.

THE IDEA

When to use it: When a major decision is needed.

Summary: Decisions are the footfalls of progress: they can be quick or slow, large or small, easy or risky, simple or arduous, but they're the vital components of success. The best decisions provide organisations with certainty and decisiveness; a clear focus on priorities; opportunities; the means to implement plans and strategy; greater revenues, lower costs, increased shareholder value – and long-term growth and prosperity. Decisions provide individuals with a framework for action – ensuring that effort is not misguided or wasted – and security and relief from the fear of inaction, indecision and uncertainty.

Decisions are often mistakenly seen as being either right or wrong, ignoring the fact that often what matters most is making the best decision from a set of choices. In certain instances all of the available decisions may be right, or they may all be flawed; the important point is to select the best available option.

A rational approach to decision making relies on a set of sequential steps and techniques: the decision-making process. This rational route involves:

continued overleaf

continued

1 assessing the situation;

2 defining the critical issues;

3 specifying the decision;

4 evaluating options and making the decision;

5 implementing the decision;

6 monitoring the decision and making adjustments as events unfold.

DESCRIPTION

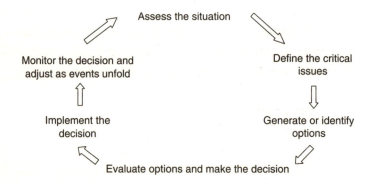

Assessing the situation

It's important to ask the right questions: What's the decision trying to achieve. What are the problems and what does the decision concern?

Consider whether the decision relates to an underlying issue or whether it's the result of an isolated event. Generic decisions need to be addressed consistently and if the problem is one that's recurred (or is likely to recur), then an 'off the shelf' solution will suffice. If the problem is unique, then unique thinking is demanded.

Defining the critical issues (and objectives)

Again, this involves asking the right questions and collecting – and comprehending – relevant information. It's often difficult to define a clear objective when there are a number of competing priorities, but there are several possible approaches.

Decide which objective offers the greatest potential benefits or which is the most important. One technique is to ask *why* it's important. What are the benefits? Also, refer to existing policies or plans (for example, a strategic business plan) to see what objective offers the greatest overall benefit. Next, consider seeking the views of others and building a consensus about the objective. Finally, test hypotheses and ideas by asking: 'If this was the objective, what would be the likely decision and what would be the possible outcome?'

Generating or evaluating options

Developing multiple options requires mental flexibility and imagination. Some of the more concrete ways of going about this include analysing the information and reviewing the possible paths to the desired outcome. Also useful are seeking the views of others, brainstorming ideas and using creativity and conceptual thinking to imagine possible scenarios and solutions.

Evaluating options and making the decision

Evaluate the available options by asking several questions.

- **What are the risks and potential barriers to success?**
- **How attractive are the options?**
- **Which decisions are feasible? (Also, could feasible options be synthesised into one decision?)**
- **When is action required?**
- **What action might be needed to keep options open for the future?**

Remember that the decision needs to be in line with the objective(s) and overall strategy, and the decision should be consistent with other decisions, policies and values. When reaching a decision, it can help to work backwards from the desired solution to find the decision most likely to bring it about – in other words, 'reverse engineering' the solution.

Implementing the decision

It's essential that practical aspects of the decision are appreciated: where, how and when the objective will be realised. Executing the decision is the most time-consuming and critical phase, and demands flexibility and un-flagging attention. The likelihood of success is increased if you:

■ **ask who will make it happen, who's responsible and what's their incentive? There's little point in making decisions if they're unworkable or misunderstood;**
■ **Communicate – make sure that people understand their roles and are engaged and capable of doing what needs to be done.**

Monitoring the decision – and making adjustments as events unfold

Making a decision – and then sticking with it – is often important, but this needs to be tempered with an ability to recognise when the situation has moved on and a new decision is required. There are two certainties: decisions will rely on and be influenced by fallible people, and decisions are made in a changing environment. Therefore, the implementation of the decision must be monitored, so reporting procedures should be built into the process. As circumstances change, and mistakes made, solutions can be perfected. Remember, the final outcome is what's important, rather than initial success.

How will you monitor the implementation of the decision? What will success look like?

DEFUSING TENSIONS (ACKNOWLEDGE, ASK, ANSWER)

What's the best way to defuse tensions or emotional outbursts? These may not occur often but when they do, the experience can catch even the best leader off-guard. This technique provides a ready-made refuge or response that will help improve the situation and achieve immediate progress.

THE IDEA

When to use it: This simple approach is invaluable during appraisals, enabling leaders to influence people (especially if they're being aggressive). The advantages are that it balances warmth with dominance and challenge with support.

Summary: The best leaders are flexible and capable of dealing with a broad range of different situations, issues and people. This includes the ability to defuse tensions and provide assertive leadership that's both warm and challenging.

DESCRIPTION

First, start by acknowledging the question, enquiry or statement, opinion and the questioner. This should be done in a way that minimises defensiveness. When acknowledging, it's useful to recognise the strength of feeling whilst also thinking about the issue. At this stage, this means neither agreeing nor disagreeing. For example, explicitly recognise the other person's strength of feeling ('I can see this is important to you…clearly you have strong feelings').

The next step is to ask – questioning the other person so that you probe, explore and fully understand:

■ **the question, enquiry or statement;**
■ **the issue at hand (this may be obscured, at least partially);**
■ **the reasoning behind his or her decision or point of view.**

'Asking' ensures that you understand the other person's motivations, adjusting your behaviour appropriately without simply accepting an issue at face value.

Once you've acknowledged the situation and taken time to explore and fully understand it, answer the question if you can (or set out a process for answering the question).

DEVELOPING BUSINESS RELATIONSHIPS

Despite their vital importance, relationships are often taken for granted. This can be a mistake: relationships, whether at work or elsewhere in life, benefit from being actively considered and nurtured. This can require nothing more than a few simple principles.

THE IDEA

When to use it: To improve understanding or teamwork and build relationships.

Summary: By giving greater priority to the quality of relationships, internally with colleagues and externally with customers and others, businesses will prosper. Several simple principles and techniques will help to ensure success.

DESCRIPTION

Most of us are taught how to build relationships when we're children; the problem seems to be that some of us forget the essentials as we grow older. Several simple rules can help (with each issue, consider where you can improve or do more).

- **Display empathy and genuine warmth. This means being supportive, open, positive, constructive and engaging – not simply 'friendly'.**
- **Remember that actions really are as important as words. Dependability, consideration and effort can go a long way to building a relationship. So, deliver what you say you will and treat others as you would wish to be treated.**
- **Actively listen and question. This helps build understanding and develop a bond that is both genuine and informed.**
- **Be confident and self-aware. This means being challenging, in control, confident, strong, authoritative and direct. It also means**

understanding how your behaviour affects others. Also, consider why people should (or do) respect you. Understand your own motivation and objectives.

- **Display assertive behaviour.** Combine appropriate levels of challenge and support.
- **Build trust** by being diligent and consistent, acting with integrity and sincerity.
- **Be considerate and realistic.** Understand who you're dealing with; take time to find out how they work and what motivates them.
- **Be patient, calm and controlled.** Remember that trust is time sensitive and fragile – it takes time and attention to develop.
- **Show your passion.** People generally respond well to effort, energy, commitment and virtue, so show yours.
- **Be clear and honest** – without hidden agendas.

DEVELOPING INFLUENCE (THE THOMAS-KILMANN CONFLICT INSTRUMENT)

Influencing – whether you're giving feedback or selling a product or idea – requires an understanding of how your behaviour affects others.

THE IDEA

When to use it: When the coachee's issue relates to a need to assert their views, persuade others, give feedback, get people engaged, handle a difficult situation or overcome conflict.

Summary: All individuals have their own personality – the result both of nature and nurture – and this remains largely unchanged. However, behaviour is different: it's flexible and capable of being developed and enhanced.

- **It's useful to consider behaviour (yours and others) in terms of warmth or coldness, dominance or submissiveness.**
- **Warm means being supportive, open, positive, empathetic, constructive and engaging – not simply 'friendly'.**
- **Cold means being suspicious, detached, not focused on people or relationships.**
- **Dominant means being challenging, in control, confident, strong, authoritative and direct.**
- **Submissive means subduing your own thoughts or actions for something or someone else.**

DESCRIPTION

The diagram below (the assertiveness model) highlights different types of behaviour (see Kenneth Wayne Thomas, *Thomas-Kilmann Conflict Mode Instrument*, published by CPP Inc, 2002).

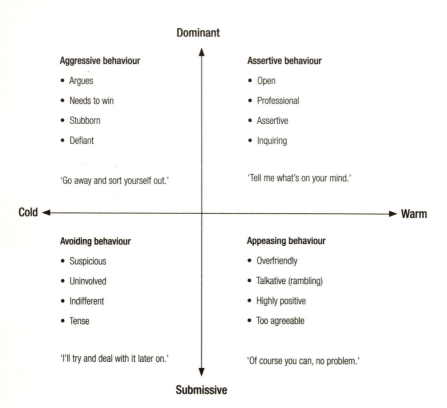

Dominant

Aggressive behaviour
- Argues
- Needs to win
- Stubborn
- Defiant

'Go away and sort yourself out.'

Assertive behaviour
- Open
- Professional
- Assertive
- Inquiring

'Tell me what's on your mind.'

Cold ← → **Warm**

Avoiding behaviour
- Suspicious
- Uninvolved
- Indifferent
- Tense

'I'll try and deal with it later on.'

Appeasing behaviour
- Overfriendly
- Talkative (rambling)
- Highly positive
- Too agreeable

'Of course you can, no problem.'

Submissive

Aggressive: dominant and cold behaviour

When dealing with aggressive behaviour, the best approach is to:

- **increase your dominance to match their high dominance levels;**
- **ensure that you're demonstrating behaviour that's assertive and warm rather than aggressive;**
- **use open questions to generate understanding;**
- **use body language and tone of voice to increase your dominance levels.**

You may also want to consider challenging and confronting the reasons behind the behaviour, with clear examples.

Avoiding: cold and submissive behaviour

When dealing with avoiding behaviour, the first priority is to get people engaged. Useful techniques include:

- **displaying lower dominance and higher warmth;**
- **using open questions aimed at making them feel secure;**
- **softening body language and intonation while continuing to smile.**

Appeasing: warm and submissive behaviour

When dealing with appeasing individuals, it can help to:

- **stay focused to keep them on track;**
- **use open questions that appeal to their social needs but temper these with closed questions when they waffle;**
- **ask summary questions to maintain clarity and focus;**
- **use their name if you're interrupting.**

Assertive: warm and dominant behaviour

When dealing with conflict, it can help to be assertive and encourage others to be assertive as well. Consider how easy it is to warm up behaviour: why and when is it not easy? Why do we, as individuals, not behave in an assertive manner? What is it that hinders supportive and challenging behaviour? Finally, what are the most important questions for you to ask?

DEVELOPING INNOVATION

How can you encourage coachees to be more creative or innovative? Helping people to see things differently attracts the best employees and increases the distinctiveness and value of a business. Innovation can be encouraged in a variety of practical ways.

THE IDEA

When to use it: To help coaches to build a culture of innovation, develop a new idea or way of working, exploit an opportunity or resolve a problem.

Summary: Organisations that struggle to be innovative often do so because ideas get stifled in their infancy by an excessive rush to judgement and analysis. Having the right kind of processes for generating ideas and innovation is important – but processes aren't enough. Innovative organisations also have a general environment and culture that values and fosters innovation, and this culture can be established by applying a range of practical techniques.

DESCRIPTION

Understand when innovation thrives and create the right conditions

There are five catalysts for successful innovation. Which of these could be improved in your business or team? How could this be achieved?

- **Consciousness.** All the employees know the goals of the organisation and believe they can play a part in achieving them.
- **Multiplicity (or diversity).** Teams and groups contain a wide and creative mix of skills, experiences, backgrounds and ideas.
- **Connectivity.** Relationships are strong and trusting and are actively encouraged and supported within and across teams and functions.

- **Accessibility.** Doors and minds are open; everyone in the organisation has access to resources, time and decision-makers.
- **Consistency.** Commitment to innovation runs throughout the organisation and is built into processes and leadership style.

Generate creative options, ideas and solutions

Some of the most popular ways to generate problem-solving ideas are described below.

- **Heuristics:** using experience to guide future plans and decisions. Characterised by flexibility and tentativeness rather than force or certainty, decisions are adapted and adjusted, as events develop, all the while guided by a specific set of values. Because of this, heuristic methods work best in situations where structured or systematic decision-making methods can't be applied, perhaps because the situation is completely new. Core principles (such as meeting customer needs) combined with experience, can be applied quickly and flexibly to find a solution.
- **Mind mapping** is an approach that organises thoughts and ideas into a structured form from which patterns and new approaches emerge or crystallise. Mind maps help to clarify issues as well as sharing and communicating ideas. A starting point is grouping issues into specific categories. Also, displaying ideas in diagrammatic form can highlight relationships between ideas.
- **Vertical and lateral thinking** is a systematic approach to creativity provided by the popular author Edward de Bono. He distinguishes between vertical thinking, bounded by logic and linear thinking, and lateral thinking that cuts across normal boundaries and processes. De Bono's view is that some techniques are inadequate for solving many problems: in these situations, lateral thinking is useful as it combines ideas and concepts that haven't previously been brought together. Also, lateral thinking removes binding assumptions by asking: *What if?*
- **Questioning** is useful as it helps to generate alternatives. This must happen in a supportive environment and is the essential

first step in breaking traditional thinking. It often helps to question established logic, asking *why?* alongside *why not?* Questioning the limits of existing processes can stimulate new ideas.

■ **Brainstorming** encourages people to give vent to all of their ideas on a specific topic, usually led by a facilitator, in an atmosphere of constructive suggestion rather than criticism, discussion or even comment. After ideas have been generated, they're discussed, explored and prioritised – often, elements of different suggestions then lead to new solutions being created. However, it's only with the adoption of several important principles that it works:

- quantity matters – generate as many ideas as possible. Quality is secondary to the quantity of ideas. The quality of each idea can be assessed later.
- suspend judgement so that participants feel free to contribute without fear that their ideas will be torpedoed by others.
- freewheel and encourage every idea, even those that may seem wild and silly. The ideas that at first seem outlandish can be the ones of greatest brilliance.
- cross-fertilise so participants can build upon each other's ideas. This is how brainstorming becomes truly productive.
- don't rush to judgement. Allow time between the generation of ideas and the evaluation process. A methodical process of elimination should be used to select the optimal solution. Set the criteria on which to rate the ideas generated. This helps to whittle down the ideas to a few promising solutions.

Apply creative techniques when time is short

■ Trying first (and asking for forgiveness later!).
■ Testing or piloting an idea.
■ Ensuring that teams are as varied and diverse as possible.
■ Seeking external input.
■ Reducing – and virtually eliminating – hierarchy.

- Involving people, generating a sense of play and working without boundaries.
- Being flexible about working arrangements.
- Accepting that it is all right to try and fail.
- Imposing a deadline, while allowing some time for people to be creative.

Develop solutions quickly using deep dive prototyping

A deep dive combines brainstorming and prototyping. These form an approach that can be used to help move a business forward. A deep dive can be completed in an hour, a day or a week. The main stages in the deep dive process are:

1 building a diverse and varied team;
2 defining the challenge;
3 visiting experts;
4 sharing ideas;
5 brainstorming and voting;
6 developing a fast prototype;
7 testing and refining the prototype;
8 focusing on the prototype and producing a final solution.

DISNEY CREATIVITY STRATEGY

This technique helps change perceptions. It's based on the creative genius of Walt Disney and his ability to think in three main styles – those of critic, realist and dreamer.

THE IDEA

When to use it: The Disney creativity strategy can be used in individual and group coaching to help people alter their perception position – seeing something from a different point of view. (For further information see Bill Capodagli, *The Disney Way: Harnessing the Management Secrets of Disney in Your Company*, published by McGraw-Hill, 2001.)

Summary: The Disney creativity strategy involves three distinct ways of thinking:

- **dreamer – the person for whom all things are possible;**
- **realist – the person who sorts things out;**
- **critic – the person who challenges or questions the parts that don't fit.**

DESCRIPTION

The participant goes into all three roles, in the indicated sequence. Each stage requires them to adopt a different approach.

About the three roles

The dreamer takes the view that 'I want to...'. The coachee takes the role of the dreamer and answers the following questions.

- **Why are you doing this?**
- **What is the purpose?**
- **What are the payoffs?**
- **How will you know you have them?**

- Where do you want to be in the future?
- Who do you want to be or be like?
- What topics do you want to consider?

The realist is the next role for the coachees, where they focus on 'How to...'. They need to establish an action plan with time-frames, progress checks and milestones, as well as agreeing evidence and test procedures. In this role, the coachees ask themselves the following questions.

- What will you do?
- How, specifically, will the idea be implemented?
- How will you know if the goal has been achieved?
- Who else is involved?
- What are the time constraints or resource issues?
- When will each phase be implemented?
- When will the overall goal be completed?
- Where will each phase be carried out?

The critic is the final role, in which the coachees challenge or probe the proposed plan or solution and answer these questions.

- How do all the elements fit together?
- What elements appear unbalanced?
- What parts don't fit with the overall objective of the project?
- What parts of the project are underdeveloped?
- How possible is this within the time frame?
- Why is each step necessary?

Using the Disney creativity strategy

Walt Disney was rumoured to use different rooms in his house for different aspects of his creative process. The following steps are designed to help coachees use this technique.

1 Select a problem – it can be small or large. Don't start evaluating the problem yet.

2 Standing in a 'neutral' space, mark three sections of the floor as three distinct areas: dreamer, realist and critic. (It's useful to label each of the spaces.)

3 Think of a time when you were really creative, when your dreamer was making some very creative choices. Step into the dreamer position and relive that time. When you finish, step back into the neutral space.

4 Think of a time when you were realistic about a plan and it was implemented successfully. It might be your own plan or somebody else's. As you recall this time, step into the realist space and relive the experience. Again, step back into neutral space when you finish.

5 Next, recall a time when you criticised a plan in a constructive way and saw weaknesses as well as strengths and identified problems. Again, it might be your plan or someone else's. As you recall this time, step into the critic space and relive the experience. Step back into the neutral space.

This helps coachees to fix *dreamer*, *realist* (or planner) and *critic* in their mind so they can apply them to the problem.

6 Consider the problem you want to work with and step into the dreamer space. Let your mind wander freely. This is an ideas space and there's no room for the realist and critic. Don't let reality come into your thoughts.

7 Now step into the realist space and consider the plan you have dreamed about. This is about organising ideas to put it into practice. What would need to happen to make it real? How could you do it?

8 Next, step into the critic space and assess the plan. What are the strengths and weaknesses? Is anything missing? What do others get out of it? What do you get out of it? What else is needed?

9 Step back into the dreamer space again and modify your dreams in the light of the new information from the realist and critic.

10 Continue to go round the three positions until the plan works in all three positions.

EIGHT PRINCIPLES OF MOTIVATION

Helping people feel motivated and engaged with their work is a complex skill and leaders often fail to understand just how difficult it is. Several practical principles can help.

THE IDEA

When to use it: Always – creating a motivating environment is something that needs to happen constantly; it can't suddenly be switched on. If you wait until people are feeling uncertain or demotivated, then it's too late.

Summary: Undoubtedly, people are motivated by a complex array of different factors; so, for example, the 'carrot and stick' approach is only one of many motives governing action. Threats or promises of more money are blunt instruments (or 'nuclear' options) that are surprisingly limited. An individual's strength of motivation is affected by the expectations of outcomes from certain actions, but it's also strengthened by other factors such as the individual's preferred outcome conditions in the working environment, as well as individuals' own perceptions and fears. These factors are reflected in the eight principles of motivation.

1 **Be motivated yourself.**

2 **Select people who are highly motivated.**

3 **Treat each person as an individual.**

4 **Set realistic and challenging targets.**

5 **Remember that progress motivates.**

6 **Create a motivating environment.**

7 **Provide fair rewards.**

8 **Give recognition.**

DESCRIPTION

Three factors affecting leaders' success at motivation are:

■ **understanding what motivates individuals to act** – this is fundamental to engaging people and focusing their efforts. Motives are inner needs or desires and these can be consciously known to individuals or buried at an unconscious level. Motives can also be mixed, with several clustered around a primary motive;

■ **understanding the external environment** – different influences, such as the needs of the team or the desire to avoid a difficult situation later, often need to be understood by the leader;

■ **the role of leaders,** who must themselves be completely self-motivated, is also a key element in motivating others.

The factors below affect the ability of leaders to apply the eight principles of motivation (ask your coachee: which areas could be improved in your situation?).

Be motivated yourself. Leadership requires self-motivation in order to set a clear example of the level of effort and commitment that is required from others, understand the causes of motivation and overcome any obstacles.

Select people who are highly motivated. Understanding individuals' motivation starts right at the beginning of the selection interviews. People may often be motivated but their motivation needs to be appropriate to the requirements of the job. For example, not everybody is motivated to sell or become a salesperson – their motivation may lie elsewhere.

Treat each person as an individual. When motivating, it's wrong to assume that everyone will respond in the same way to the same stimulus or promise. Indeed, people may often react against being viewed the same as others. Everyone will have their own feelings resulting from individual perspectives, values, experiences and personality, and these will affect their motivation. The more leaders understand what motivates specific individuals, the more success they will have in focusing those people.

Set realistic and challenging targets. When leading others, it's often easy to set targets that the individuals just don't buy into, resulting in failure and demotivation. The key is to understand the needs of the team, task and individuals and set targets that are challenging but realistic, and which the individuals can engage with.

Remember that progress motivates. Achieving success is a great motivator and because of this the best teams often celebrate their successes. There's a virtuous spiral that occurs when success is achieved as it reinforces confidence and motivation.

Create a motivating environment. Leaders have to create the right conditions in which people can thrive and this means removing obstacles such as bureaucracy, policies or procedures that can reduce motivation; making sure that individuals aren't frustrated by a lack of necessary resources; understanding any training and development needs; monitoring progress – coaching and guiding where necessary – and acknowledging achievements.

Provide fair rewards. They encourage people and can take a number of forms; for example, promotion, additional resources or responsibilities, as well as pay and benefits.

Give recognition. Recognition of successes achieved or effort involved will go a long way to ensuring that the team members' motivation is sustained. Leaders need to maintain their team members' momentum for their ongoing success.

Finally, there is a ninth rule of motivation that should not be overlooked.

Make clear your intent. Increasingly, individuals feel that they have been led by people at the top of organisations who have had their own agendas as a priority, rather than those that they lead. The global credit crunch, recession and failing companies, together with the hunt for CEOs and leaders to blame, testify to this attitude. People need to be clear about the intent of those who lead.

EMPOWERMENT

Empowerment is a way of releasing the creative power that team-members have, not for one specific task but in their job as a whole.

THE IDEA

When to use it: Always – it's vital when leading people that they feel responsible and in control of their contribution and achievements. This will help tap into the talents that people have and ensure that each individual's full capabilities are employed.

Summary: Empowerment is based on the belief that the full capabilities of team members are frequently underused and, given the right work environment and level of responsibility, people will start to make a much greater, positive contribution. When empowering team members, you're letting them get on with the job entirely: they're both responsible and accountable, within certain agreed boundaries. Empowerment means:

- **letting each member of the team get on with the job;**
- **letting those team-members closest to customers (both within and outside the organisation) take decisions themselves;**
- **removing obstacles and unnecessary bureaucracy;**
- **encouraging and enabling people to put their ideas for improvement into practice.**

DESCRIPTION

Empowerment requires the leader to:

- **set a clear, unambiguous direction and ensure that people remain on course;**

- retain a full understanding of what's happening;
- offer support, open doors, and clear the way for action without taking over from those delegated to do the job;
- make decisions which others can't, either because of lack of time, information or knowledge;
- continuously assess performance, reward progress and support individual and team development;
- build trust through shared success; share information and knowledge whenever it's possible to do so.

Several principles will help you (as a leader) empower members of your team.

- **Understand what you mean by empowerment.** Make sure you know what you want to get out of empowering your team; let your colleagues and senior managers know your plans, and check that their expectations meet your own.
- **Assess the barriers to empowerment** – what are they (for example, people may fear responsibility or there may be a culture of blame) and how can they be overcome?
- **Build the right culture within your team** – some organisations have cultures that are more conducive to empowerment than others. If you're serious about empowering your team to make their own decisions and take greater responsibility, then you should promote trust and respect, remove a climate of fear and blame, and focus on the needs of the task, team and each individual.
- **Establish the boundaries** – empowerment provides people with greater autonomy and responsibility but it's vital to agree and set clear limits. This may include, for example, agreeing expenditure limits. Also, be prepared to have these boundaries tested: only then will clear limits be established.
- **Communicate and win support** – you'll need to raise awareness among those around you of what's involved in empowerment; this may involve reassuring some, selling the benefits and winning the support of others.

■ **Make sure that people have the right skills and resources to take control** – review what each member of your team does now and what they're likely to be doing in future. This is an opportunity to alter and update job descriptions; assess training needs, and make sure that your team has sufficient resources.

■ **Agree objectives and performance measures** – empowerment is about giving people the responsibility and resources to complete tasks on an ongoing basis. As with delegation, it's not about dumping work on people and leaving them, and it requires you to agree the necessary level of speed, accuracy and cost-efficiency.

■ **Monitor developments.** You'll need to make people aware of what's happening and try to secure early 'wins' that highlight the value of the process. Monitor developments and iron out any difficulties, particularly in the early days, but take care not to interfere or undermine the process.

It's important to understand that when you empower your team members you're giving them a complete job and area of responsibility, within definite boundaries, rather than delegating one specific task or project.

ENHANCING MOTIVATION

Different people are motivated by different things. Understanding what motivates individuals is an important part of helping them to improve their skills and realise their potential. It also enables the coach to energise an individual.

THE IDEA

When to use it: When you need to understand what motivates someone.

Summary: Research suggests that 12 outcomes affect an individual's motivation. A key challenge for any coach is to accurately understand what motivates another person, appreciating which of these 12 outcomes are most significant for that particular person.

DESCRIPTION

Twelve outcomes affect an individual's motivation. Once these motivations have been recognised, the next challenge is to increase or maintain motivation by matching your behaviour to an individual's preferred outcome. Techniques for accomplishing this are described below.

Source of motivation	Do	Don't
Independence	• Provide privacy and favour individual rather than group interaction. • Listen, don't tell and ask for advice – participative management is important. • Emphasise similarity and congruence between personal and organisational goals. • Provide opportunities for leadership in the organisation.	• Recommend or breed conformity. • Fail to give positive reinforcement.
Recognition	• Ensure that recognition is sincere and develops over time (a desire for recognition is almost universal). • Balance constructive criticism with praise. • Provide opportunities to participate in decisions, when appropriate.	• Devalue recognition by being insincere. • Ignore an individual who is motivated by recognition.

Source of motivation	Do	Don't
Achievement	• Be available for advice but help only when asked. • Encourage individuals to set their own goals. • Compare results with goals and highlight specific rather than general issues. • Provide new challenges.	• Supervise too closely or impose your own standards. • Set goals. • Expect conformity.
Leisure time	• Consider how leisure time can be enhanced by improving performance.	• Ignore work schedules and deadlines. • Intrude on leisure time.
Power	• Give individual attention, listening rather than telling. • Recognise when individuals ask for feedback but don't really want it. • Help individuals understand that they're needed.	• Fail to give recognition or criticise too heavily. • Fail to highlight how individuals are succeeding.
Prestige	• Encourage individuals to get involved in a range of activities. • Support the individuals, introducing them to people, resources and situations that will advance their prospects. • Provide genuine and sincere praise – recognise that if praise is given to a group, it may limit an individual's growth.	• Ignore the significance of the trappings of success.
Money	• Link objectives with commission and remuneration. • Consider introducing a performance-related bonus system.	• Don't ignore the significance of money and other forms of remuneration.
Pressure	• Agree intermediate and final deadlines. • Provide focus and set challenging goals. • Encourage a work–life balance. • Be patient and provide continued support and reassurance.	• Overreact. • Ignore causes of concern.
Self-esteem	• Encourage people with low esteem by recognising achievements. • Avoid threats and set realistic goals. • Set challenging goals and delegate both responsibility and authority.	• Ignore the need for guidance, independence, recognition and support.
Family life	• Show genuine interest and acceptance of family life. • Recognise the value of social interaction.	• Become over-involved in family issues or play at being a counsellor.

Source of motivation	Do	Don't
Security	• Ensure consistency. • Provide supervision in a predictable, comfortable way. • Set goals.	• 'Rock the boat' without careful consideration of the likely consequences.
Personal growth	• Channel activities and effort. • Focus on an individual's feelings. • Provide specific rather than general suggestions for progress.	• Ignore the need for recognition, practical support and positive reinforcement.

These techniques are useful for helping coaches to understand and support the motivations of their clients. They're also a valuable, proven method that may help clients to understand and encourage the teams that they lead.

FORCE FIELD ANALYSIS

Force field analysis is one of the most effective ways of assessing the factors influencing a situation or decision. It appeals to coachees who have a logical and analytical preference or approach.

THE IDEA

When to use it: To identify, assess and understand the relative significance of a broad range of conflicting influences. Useful when someone is 'stuck' in a decision-making process.

Summary: Force field analysis is a core coaching technique that can be widely applied in a range of situations – notably for decision-making and problem solving. Its value lies in identifying and understanding the relative significance of several issues – positive and negative – affecting a situation or decision.

DESCRIPTION

Originally developed by social psychologist Kurt Lewin, force field analysis provides a practical way to assess a range of factors (forces) that are influencing a situation or decision (see Lewin, K., *Resolving Social Conflicts and Field Theory in Social Science*, Washington, DC: American Psychological Association, 1997). It looks at the forces that are either *driving* movement towards a goal or *blocking* (resisting or hindering) movement. The principle is used widely the fields of social science, psychology, organisational development, process management and change management.

In this example of force field analysis, the issue being considered is whether to change career.

Forces for change	Score
More money	8
Better work–life balance	7
Better long-term prospects	5
More stimulating and varied	4
Greater responsibility	6
Greater emphasis on developing new skills	2
Total	**32**

CHANGE CAREER

Forces against change	Score
Sunk cost – already started current career	2
Effort required to find the right job	3
Competitiveness of the job market	3
Lack of relevant experience	5
Concerns about self-confidence	7
Fear of failure	7
Total	**27**

1 State your plan or proposal for change in the middle.

2 List all of the forces *for* change in one column and all the forces *against* change in the other column.

3 Assign a score to each force, from 1 (weak or insignificant) to 10 (strong or highly significant). If it helps, include arrows to show the relative strength of each force.

4 Total the forces for and against the decision.

5 Review and discuss:

■ **the list of factors** – these should be as comprehensive as possible and include anything that, in the individual's mind, affects the change, either 'for' or 'against'. Are all the relevant issues listed? How does the individual feel about each issue? Are there any surprise inclusions or omissions?

■ **the ratings for each factor** – what's the reason for assigning a force a particular score? What's the trend – is the factor becoming more or less significant?

■ **the totals for and against the change.** In the example above, the forces for a change in career (totalling 32) are greater than the forces against (27). So, on the surface it looks like a change is desirable. Simply realising this fact can help to bring clarity to a situation that may otherwise be quite confusing. Are these totals accurate? Are they surprising? What do they imply to the individual about the change?

■ **How to achieve progress** – are there ways that the individual can harness the forces *for* change? Perhaps more importantly, how can the forces *against* the change be countered or overcome? This can then lead into a discussion about goals and priorities.

6 How to avoid potential pitfalls.

■ Force field analysis works when there's a simple decision or situation to assess, not when there are competing options.

■ The input must come from coachees: it must be their list of issues, not yours or anyone else's.

■ Input must be comprehensive and thoughtful. An incomplete list or inaccurate ratings will undermine the activity.

Force field analysis assesses current reality. Often, to be fully effective, this improved understanding should lead to a discussion about goals.

THE FOUR STAGES OF ACHIEVING EMOTIONAL COMMITMENT

Obtaining commitment and engaging people with a business strategy or task can be achieved by taking them through four emotional stages.

THE IDEA

When to use it: When you need to develop or implement a new idea, decision or plan.

Summary: There are four emotional stages which you can take people through when you need to implement a new decision.

DESCRIPTION

Obtaining commitment and engaging people with the strategy can be achieved by taking people through four emotional stages:

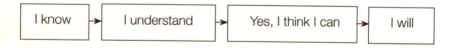

I know → I understand → Yes, I think I can → I will

Explain the issue. Explaining the issue's context and relevance is the first, essential step. This provides valuable information without necessarily generating commitment.

Highlight the issue's significance. The next stage builds on this by generating clear understanding of why the decision is significant for the organisation and, in particular, why it's important to individuals and what it means for them.

Generate commitment. The next part of the process of generating commitment is to make the decision attainable. This can be accomplished by achieving early victories that generate momentum and involvement.

Instil belief. Finally, getting people to believe that they can achieve success can develop commitment. To do this:

- involve people in key decisions early;
- divide the decision or project into tangible, practical steps;
- make people feel involved and genuinely committed, for example, by celebrating successes and fostering teamwork.

FUNDAMENTAL INTERPERSONAL RELATIONS ORIENTATION (FIRO-B)

Originated by Will Schutz in the early 1950s, the FIRO-B (**f**undamental **i**nterpersonal **r**elations **o**rientation – **b**ehaviour) test assesses the ways in which a person typically interacts with other people.

THE IDEA

When to use it: When you want to better understand how coachees interact with people, and how their behaviour might be interpreted.

Summary: FIRO-B is based on the view that three aspects of interpersonal relations explain most human interaction. These are *inclusion, control* and *affection*. These categories measure how much interaction a person wants in the areas of socialising, leadership and responsibilities, and more intimate personal relations.

DESCRIPTION

Will Schutz, originator of the FIRO theory and of the FIRO-B questionnaire, recognised that 'people need people' and that more specifically 'people need people to receive from and give to in varying degrees' and in three specific areas.

Inclusion

This is about how much coachees want to include and involve other people in their activities, and how much attention and recognition they want from others.

The advantages of inclusion are a preference to interact, mingle, communicate, belong, display companionship, be collegial and collaborate. With inclusion there's no neutral ground – you're either in or out, one of us or one of them – and not being included usually feels bad to some extent. In fact, negative elements include exclusion, isolation, loneliness, detachment, being withdrawn and feeling abandoned or ignored.

Control

This is about the way that coachees usually react to the need to take charge of situations or being directed by others. It includes issues such as authority, responsibility, decision making and influence on others.

The positive aspects include: authority, dominance, influence, control and leadership, while the negative elements are rebellion, resistance, submissiveness and even anarchy. For example, in a group discussion someone seeking inclusion will want to participate and be prominent in the discussion, whereas someone seeking control will want to be the 'winner' (or on the same side as the winner).

Affection

This describes a coachee's close interpersonal relationships, for example, with good friends or someone who they work with. Positive aspects include love, an emotional connection, warmth, positive feelings and friendship, whereas negative aspects are coolness, distance or dislike.

Crucially, those behaviours that we initiate are termed *expressed behaviours*, while those that we'd like others to initiate are *wanted behaviours*. The FIRO-B questionnaire highlights a person's current preferences for expressed and wanted behaviours, inclusion, control and affection, on 0–9 point scales where 9 is high.

For further information see *The Interpersonal Underworld* by Will Schutz (Science and Behaviour Books, Inc, 1966).

GETTING PEOPLE ENGAGED

People like to be engaged and involved and if this happens, they do better and go further. (The opposite of engagement can be viewed as 'mushroom management', where people are fed dirt and kept in the dark.) The Gallup organisation has conducted research for many of the world's top-performing businesses which has shown that engaged employees are more effective. According to Jim Clifton, Gallup's Chairman and CEO, speaking about the 'Next Generation of Leadership': 'The old rules still apply. But to win in the new world, leaders must understand their constituents' state of mind'.

So, how do you build engagement?

THE IDEA

When to use it: When someone is struggling to get members of their team engaged with an issue or situation.

Summary: Building engagement starts within – meaning that you need to genuinely want to engage with other people, understanding and valuing interaction.

DESCRIPTION

The questions below are designed to help the coachee develop the right approach in their own mind, as well as moving on to the more practical aspects of engagement.

1 **Develop a personal understanding of engagement. What does engagement mean to you? Why might it be of value to your organisation, your team and yourself?**

   It may help you to reflect on a time when a project or situation involving several people worked really well and people were engaged. What were the factors or conditions that lead to this engagement? What was achieved by people who were enthused and engaged? How did they work and what were their accomplishments?

2 **Understand your relationships and constituents.** Who are the people that you need to engage with? Are your relationships with these people strong enough for you to succeed? Crucially, how can you build and strengthen these relationships?

To help you answer these questions, it may help to reflect on a successful interaction or conversation that you had with someone. How did it go? What was the pattern and tone of the interaction? What was the outcome? How did it feel? What would you do differently next time?

3 **Decide the best approach.** What type of engagement would work well in a specific situation? The options vary considerably but may include, for example: telling people information; selling ideas, information or decisions to people; including people in certain, clearly-defined aspects of a situation, decision or process (for example, delegating specific tasks), or collaborating with people across a wide range of activities, seeking and benefiting from their views and generally working together and 'co-creating'.

Decide the scope and boundaries of engagement. How engaged – and in what way – do you want people to be with a specific situation or decision?

GIVING UNBIASED FEEDBACK

Giving unbiased feedback is an essential aspect of coaching. High-quality feedback is one of the hardest things to get from those who are likely to be affected by us, and it is difficult to give to those around us that we will be affected by. Quite naturally, we do not wish to offend others or be offended by them; as a result, we often let relationships disintegrate, rather than giving feedback to the other person about what we would like them to stop doing or how we interpret what they are doing or saying. So, how do you give valuable, unbiased feedback?

THE IDEA

When to use it: Every time you meet a client, you will be 'receiving' him or her for the first time, just as other people will. Notice what you experience. What specifically causes you to feel what you do?

Summary: High-performance teams are able to offer feedback to each other because they have enough trust to know that feedback given in the right way is imparted with a genuine wish to make things better. In coaching, however, feedback is given without judgement and is modelled from the effects of transference and counter-transference. Great coaches need to be able to give feedback in a way that is valuable and influential.

DESCRIPTION

What feelings are you aware of in yourself when meeting your coachee for the first time? How do their general demeanour, facial expressions and energy level affect you?

'Data' from others that produces an internal response can range from the judgement you make about whether they look warm, friendly or attractive (or not), to a huge range of other things that affect our interaction. For example:

■ **Reputation – others' beliefs about the person;**
■ **Status;**

- Height;
- Age;
- Gender – beliefs about gender roles;
- Hair – style, colour, lack of;
- Demeanour, smiles, lack of smiles, seriousness;
- Voice tone;
- Accent (in the UK, especially where accent has subtle educational and class connotations);
- Clothing – style, appropriateness, cultural influence;
- Jewellery, watch – quality and cost;
- Nationality – what stereotypes are you holding?;
- Race – what are your feelings about people other than your own racial group?;
- Cultural information.

Once you have honestly examined your responses to a coachee and checked why you may have felt a particular way, you are then able to proceed with the very valuable job of giving feedback uncoloured by your own assumptions. At the very least, you will be aware that if you operate as a coach with anyone who provokes a response in you which you find hard to control you would be better to take this into supervision or hand the client over to someone else.

GROW

The coaching conversation can be seen as having four main phases focusing on an individual's goals, reality, options and will.

THE IDEA

When to use it: To structure and focus a coaching conversation.

Summary: There are four main phases in a coaching conversation.

- **Goals. Setting goals both for the overall coaching relationship and for a particular session.**
- **Reality. Exploring the current position of the coachees: the reality of their circumstances and their concerns.**
- **Options. Generating options, strategies and action plans for achieving the goals outlined above.**
- **Will. Deciding what is to be done, by whom, how and when, and whether sufficient will and determination is present to see this through.**

This is aptly known as the GROW model, and the central element is that responsibility for setting the goals rests with the coachee.

DESCRIPTION
Goal-setting

This process gives the coach a framework around which many other tools and techniques can be used. It separates out the stages of analysis, for each issue raised by the coachee, and it allows the coachee to look at each stage in turn. An important aspect of the GROW model is that it isn't linear – the different stages can be revisited any number of times, until all the necessary information has been gathered and scrutinised. The goal, for example, may change several times before the coachee commits to a final, clear version.

It's worth noting that, in general, the greater control and involvement that coachees have in setting and achieving their goals, the more likely they are to achieve success. Conversely, the greater the level of outside influences, changing circumstances or reliance on others, then the more likely it is that coachees will fail to remain committed to their goals, seeing them as subject to circumstances largely beyond their control.

An antidote to this frequent problem – besides encouraging individuals to examine the facts, to suggest a solution or to find another route to their objective – is to help distinguish between end goals and performance goals. End goals are the ultimate objective of a coachee. They could typically be to gain promotion or additional responsibility, to complete a major project or to develop a different set of behaviours. Performance goals establish the level of performance that will help individuals to achieve their end goal. Performance goals can include such elements as quality standards, time management, production targets or feedback from other people.

Understanding the reality and options phases of the GROW model

The purpose of the reality phase is to enable coachees quickly to analyse and understand their current situation. This can include facts or figures, obstacles, resources available or people involved in the situation. The role of the coach is essentially to prompt the coachees by asking questions that uncover the reality. The coach can also help by providing information, if possible, and also by summarising the situation so far, as this will help to clarify the reality for the coachees.

The coach then needs to help the coachees see the way forward, and this is done by helping them generate and then select options. The coaches need to feel comfortable with – and committed to – the option they choose.

Deciding what is to be done – the final phase of the GROW model

Finally, the coachees need to generate a practical action plan so that they can implement their chosen option. The coach's role here is largely as a sounding board, highlighting strengths and weaknesses and offering an additional perspective that supports the coachees. The plan needs to outline the action required, focusing in particular on what, when, who and how. It should also incorporate a review and feedback process to check progress and the necessary resources and attitude to ensure success. The coach's role is to help provide these and encourage the coachees to use them.

HEAD, HEART AND GUTS: A SYSTEMIC APPROACH

To lead in today's complex, connected and volatile world, it can help leaders to view their priorities as being in several main areas: setting and implementing strategy, developing trusting relationships, consistently making decisions and doing the right thing based on personal values. Achieving this requires a balanced, integrated and systemic approach that combines the head, heart and guts.

THE IDEA

When to use it: When you want to encourage leaders to operate with a 'broader' mind and a wider perspective than ever before.

Summary: How can leaders keep pace and succeed in an increasingly fast-moving and volatile world? The answer lies with a focus on head, heart and gut. The difficulty is that leaders often rely exclusively on a single quality: data and rational analysis (head), emotional connection (heart) or courage (guts) – but not all three. Concentrating on just one of these dimensions will mean ignoring other aspects necessary for enduring success. If you rely on your analytical rigour, you may be seen as insensitive or unethical, or you may lack the ability to respond outside a narrow range of situations. If you try to create a compassionate culture, you may miss opportunities that a more strategic leader would have seen. Relying solely on the courage of your conviction and toughness may lead you to underestimate the negative consequences for the people you are trying to lead.

DESCRIPTION

More than ever before, leaders are managing complex situations and constituencies that require a broader range of leadership attributes. They are faced with decisions to which there are no 'right' solutions. They will have to learn how to *manage* paradoxes rather than try to *resolve* them. Sometimes they will have to act counterintuitively and at other times they will need to trust their instincts. Dealing with these difficult and ever-shifting situations is not possible without head, heart and guts working together.

A systemic, integrated approach to developing leadership is an effective way to prepare for a world of uncertainty and change. Today, many companies still develop their leaders the way they did when leadership demands were different. For example, they often use traditional classroom training, focusing almost exclusively on cognitive learning. Even when more effective and imaginative methods are used (such as project work or temporary assignments), the danger is that people revert to their old way of doing things when they return to the workplace. To develop capable leaders, however, organisations need to move away from this traditional approach and instead embrace a more holistic way of working.

Leadership challenges such as negotiating, making decisions and communicating require leaders to integrate and display brains, emotional intelligence and courage. The solution is to create a development process that is comprehensive, capable and intelligent.

HERON'S SIX CATEGORIES OF INTERVENTION

John Heron, a psychologist, developed a simple but comprehensive model of the six types of intervention a doctor, counsellor, therapist – or coach – could use with a patient or client.

THE IDEA

When to use it: It can be used in two ways: one for coaches, the other for coachees. It can help coachees decide how and when to intervene and help others. It also enables coaches to consider or time their approach during a coaching session.

Summary: The six types of intervention are:

- prescriptive
- informative
- confrontational
- cathartic
- catalytic
- supportive

Each type of intervention can be looked at separately during training sessions as options throughout the consultation.
(For further information see Heron, J. *Six Category Intervention Analysis*, University of Surrey, 1975.)

DESCRIPTION

Which type of intervention will work best – and what are your options?

■ **Prescriptive. In this mode the coach gives advice and may be directive (e.g. 'You need to...')**

- **Informative.** Here, the coach can be didactic, instructing or informing (e.g. 'People frequently avoid difficult conversations because they fear rejection.')
- **Confrontative.** This is confrontation but in a positive way – challenging or possibly giving direct feedback (e.g. 'You've mentioned several times how much you value that person, yet you haven't spoken to them in months.')
- **Cathartic.** In this mode the coach releases tension and encourages coachees to express their feelings (e.g. 'What do you really want to say to your colleague?')
- **Catalytic.** The coach is reflective, possibly encouraging self-directed problem solving (e.g. 'Can you say some more about that?' or 'How can you do that?')
- **Supportive.** The coach is approving, confirming or validating (e.g. 'I can understand how you feel' or 'That must have been very difficult for you.')

INSPIRING TRUST

Trust is an essential aspect of productive, positive relationships. Coachees will benefit hugely when they understand the laws of trust and what it means to be trusted.

THE IDEA

When to use it: Whenever you need to build or rebuild relationships – for example, when starting work with a new team.

Summary: Trust isn't a coat, a temporary 'quick fix' approach that we can use when it suits us and discard when we choose. It's a genuine belief system. We don't trust people for our own personal gain. We trust them because it's the right thing to do, and, in the end, we all benefit by doing the right thing.

DESCRIPTION
The principles of trust

What are the basic laws of engendering trust? What do trusted individuals do, and what do they avoid doing? It's useful to remember several important points.

- **Self trust is a critical factor in creating trust** – if you don't trust yourself, it's unlikely that others will.
- **Trust is an absolute** – there's no such thing as partial trust, it's an 'either/or'. Either it exists or it doesn't. We either trust someone or we don't.
- **Understand your personal motivation and behaviour.** People who are trusted enjoy great insight into their own patterns of behaviour and motivation. They can answer questions such as 'Why do I behave the way I do?' 'What motivates me?' 'What affects my behaviour?' Understanding these questions will enable you to deliver the core requirements of trust, such as fairness, openness, courage and the other drivers of trust. This personal insight is, of course, notoriously difficult to achieve, and

many people make a great deal of money helping others to find the answers.

■ **Waiting for people to prove their trust doesn't work.** The issue is not 'can I trust them' but 'I will trust them'. Trust is not only earned – it must be given. Remember that if you trust someone, they usually live up to it.

■ **Trust can take a long time to build and it can be destroyed in an instant**. It can take much commitment, many actions and a long time to create trust – and only one small act to destroy it.

■ **You can't create trust if you view it as a means to an end.** If you cynically try to build trust, you're unlikely to succeed. It's people who care about building relationships for their own sake, who make and keep commitments and for whom honesty and integrity are important that succeed in building trust.

■ **You can't create trust without respected values.** The values of integrity and honesty are the basis of all trusting relationships and high-trust cultures.

■ **Trust is often invisible or taken for granted.** We can fail to realise that things are going well because of trust or going badly because of the lack of it. Whilst trust is often invisible, it only exists as the result of constant actions and attention to the relationships and actions that create it. It's only when it disappears that we notice its absence. Trust's low profile status doesn't diminish its power. In fact, trust often only becomes visible when it has been lost or abused in some way.

■ **Trust requires commitment.** Trust doesn't just happen. It requires commitment, personal responsibility and vigilance.

■ **Trust relies on reciprocal relationships.** Trust centres around the virtuous cycle of 'giving and getting' interactions. Well-balanced people get psychological satisfaction from being trusted and as they're trusted more, so their trustworthiness grows.

■ **Trust opens up possibilities that can never exist without it.** Without trust, people and organisations can never be totally efficient, creative and successful, because trust allows people to try new things, disagree with others and say what they want to say.

- **Trust means understanding why people should (or do) respect you.** This means understanding what your goal is in a particular situation and how you can work with people to achieve it. Of course, it also means behaving ethically by gathering the facts and understanding where the problems lie, thinking through the issues and considering the consequences of actions. Know your obligations and understand your own motives and feelings.
- **Trust is time-sensitive, fragile and complex.** For example, a firm may be trusted by its customers but despised by its employees, and think that the situation is fine. It is not. Trust and mistrust are like water; they flow, they get everywhere and they can be more powerful than they appear at first sight. Mistrust is especially corrosive so, for example, the firm will soon find that its problems with its workforce are inevitably being transmitted to its customers.
- **Understand that the alternatives to (or substitutes for) trust are limited or non-existent.** For example, contracts and documents are no substitute for genuine trust. They may serve a purpose, but that's not creating trust and they can actually jeopardise it. The spirit of an agreement is often as important as the letter of the law.

Techniques to develop trusted relationships

The principles mentioned above help us to understand how we can create, maintain or regain trust. However, several practical actions need to be taken if we're to be regarded as trustworthy.

Avoid the power game. There's a tendency for people to prefer the pursuit of power to the pursuit of trust. It's easy to understand why: power is seen as providing control and security, whereas trust is seen as a riskier or 'softer' option. What's often forgotten is the fact that trust is much more durable, flexible and less brittle than power. It lasts and it works better.

Avoiding the power game means creating trust, and the benefits of the trust approach are stark and compelling when compared with the alternative.

Understand the characteristics of trustworthy people:

Characteristics of trustworthy people...	...and signs that they are untrustworthy
Always display the highest standards of behaviour – and encourage this in others.	Often compromise personal integrity and ethical behaviour (for example, when placed under business pressure).
Build and inspire the confidence of all stakeholders.	Infrequently take steps to build and maintain the trust of key stakeholders.
Act as role models for corporate values.	Occasionally contradict colleagues and corporate values.
Behaviour is fair and consistent, and underpins team business conduct.	Occasionally behave unreasonably, inconsistently or with a lack of respect.
Resolve issues positively and with integrity, encouraging trust between the business and stakeholders.	Occasionally undermine trust.

Understand the drivers of trust. What actions build trust? In research conducted by Jeremy Kourdi and Sally Bibb, people were asked to rate the significance of a wide range of attributes when deciding whether to trust someone. The top 10 most popular attributes are:

1 **fairness**
2 **dependability**
3 **respect**
4 **openness**
5 **courage**
6 **unselfishness**
7 **competence**
8 **supportiveness**
9 **empathy**
10 **compassion**

These are *the drivers of trust*. Understanding and delivering each of these qualities is vital if trust is to be developed. These attributes are typically what we look for when deciding whether and, quite probably, how much to trust someone.

KOTTER'S EIGHT-STAGE PROCESS FOR LEADING CHANGE

Leadership expert John Kotter studied 100 companies going through transition. By analysing their triumphs and pitfalls, he identified a number of commonly made mistakes. This led Kotter to compile the 'eight-stage process': a sequence of actions that coachees can take to ensure that changes succeed.

THE IDEA

When to use it: Whenever you need to change the way a business or team works, or when you need to help people change.

Summary: An organisation or team undergoing significant changes can pay attention to eight key steps to avoid the problems that typically capsize most attempts at transition.

DESCRIPTION

1 **Establish a sense of urgency.** Organisations frequently allow high levels of complacency to develop during times of transition. Kotter commented: 'Without motivation, people won't help and the effort goes nowhere. Executives underestimate how hard it can be to drive people out of their comfort zones.' To accept change, businesses need a 'burning platform' to remove complacency and inertia.

2 **Form a strong guiding coalition.** A group of strong, unified leaders should drive the change process and establish support throughout the entire organisation.

3 **Create a vision.** A clear sense of direction and an idea of the end result will allow efforts to be focused, organised and efficient.

4 **Communicate the vision.** The strategy and vision for change must be communicated to everyone involved. As well as holding discussions and using other forms of communication, members

of the guiding coalition should act as role models for the type of behaviours and decisions that are needed.

5 **Empower others to act on the vision.** If old procedures and obstacles remain in place during change, it will be demotivating for employees involved in the effort. So, encourage and support people to make the right changes, ideally, without always referring upwards.

6 **Plan for and create short-term victories.** Find ways to start the process and work hard to generate momentum, even in small ways. Motivate employees by continuously emphasising milestones and successes. Accentuate the positive aspects of the transition.

7 **Consolidate improvements and maintain momentum.** Rather than growing complacent as the process develops, use the credibility gained to reinvigorate and expand the changes to all areas of the company.

8 **Institutionalise the new approaches.** Anchor the changes firmly in the culture of the organisation. When changes become entrenched, they're most effective.

When planning a change process with these steps in mind, it's important to allow enough time for the full sequence of events and to carry them out in the correct order. Kotter discovered that following the change plan sequentially and patiently was fundamental to success.

- Ensure your change process has both a leader, to align, motivate and inspire the workforce, and a manager, to make a complex set of processes run smoothly and according to plan.
- Create a clear vision of the process, as well as a sequence of events that will occur, and communicate this throughout your organisation.
- Paint a compelling vision of the future and produce strategies to realise this vision.
- Understand that different types of change processes will require different skills and attributes, at different times. For example, a

crisis change process may require an emphasis on strong
leadership rather than management.
- Even successful change processes are messy and don't always
go according to plan – be ready to deal with the unexpected.

Ensure your 'guiding coalition' is unified in its objectives and that everyone
works as a team.

THE LEADERSHIP PIPELINE

The leadership pipeline is designed to develop leadership at all levels – now and for the future. It provides a practical framework for creating future leaders by planning and supporting their development.
(The principles are based on the book *The Leadership Pipeline: How to Build the Leadership-powered Company* by Ram Charan, Stephen Drotter and James Noel.)

THE IDEA

When to use it: For succession planning and to identify and develop future leaders.

Summary: The leadership pipeline provides a framework for leadership development and succession planning by:

- **explaining what success looks like at each level of management;**
- **describing how to improve skills – from newcomers to top executives;**
- **ensuring consistency across organisations;**
- **explaining how to prepare for career advancement.**

DESCRIPTION

The leadership pipeline focuses on six key transition points or challenges, each representing a major career transition. By focusing on these transitions (for example, the challenge of moving from leading people to leading leaders), individuals are better able to focus on:

- **skill requirements – the skills needed to succeed at each stage;**
- **time requirements – the priorities, timescales and work completed at each stage;**
- **work values – the things that are important to people at each stage.**

COACHING TOOLS, TECHNIQUES AND USEFUL MODELS **183**

Individuals need to understand these three aspects so that they can operate and develop successfully in their role, as well as planning and preparing for the future.

How it works

There are six stages in the leadership pipeline:

1 **self-leadership: individuals are responsible for their own effectiveness, development and results;**
2 **leading others: individuals are responsible for the work of other people;**
3 **leading managers: individuals are responsible for the work of other managers;**
4 **leading leaders: individuals are responsible for the delivery of part of a business;**
5 **leading a business: individuals are accountable for the results of a business;**
6 **leading your organisation: individuals are responsible for more than one business.**

The leadership pipeline improves the performance of individuals, teams and, consequently, the business. It meets three vital business needs. First, it provides clarity about what's required, at different leadership levels, to ensure great performance. Second, it makes the right development accessible for all, helping people understand the development that's needed at different stages of their career. Finally, it enables people to focus their development activities.

Where am I in the leadership pipeline?

The following questionnaire is a quick, easy way to give your coachees an indication of what stage they are at on the leadership pipeline. They should review their responses and read the results paragraph below that represents the majority response.

1 I typically…

a   manage my own performance.

b   manage the performance of a team.

c   manage the performance of other managers who manage teams.

d   manage and lead a business, focusing on business strategy and financial awareness.

e   manage and lead a business, building cross-business unit value, taking full accountability for P&L.

2 I typically…

a   plan my own work.

b   plan and allocate the work of others.

c   assign managerial work to managers within my team for them to plan.

d   am involved in strategic planning for the department or function in which I work.

e   define strategy and drive the business.

3 Primarily, I…

a   am responsible for my own development.

b   coach and develop a team.

c   develop managers to develop and coach their teams to support business delivery.

d   am responsible for managing longer-term talent and people development in my unit.

e   am accountable for longer-term talent and people development of the business.

4 It's important in my role that I…

a   build local relationships for personal results and benefits.

b   build relationships external to the team.

c   work horizontally across the business.

d   build networks across the organisation.

e   take accountability for internal and external stakeholder management relevant to the organisation.

5 I typically…

a   get results through personal proficiency and individual delivery.

b   get results through leading and developing others.

c   get results through setting direction and leading managers to deliver through their teams.

d   get results through creating, selling or delivering a service and setting strategy to deliver this.

e   get results through building cross-business unit value and driving the business.

RESULTS

Mostly As – Self-leadership, focusing on personal identity; developing individual expertise; learning from mentors, peers and from your manager.

Mostly Bs – Leading others, focusing on professional identity; planning, organising and integrating expertise; developing influence and inter-dependence; coaching; developing engagement and team commitment; working through others.

Mostly Cs – Leading managers, focusing on developing leadership identity; ensuring cross-functional integration; displaying vision and authority; generating organisational commitment; learning from mistakes.

Mostly Ds – Leading leaders, focusing on business identity; building reputation and authority; dealing with increasing complexity; having a pivotal role in enterprise structure; dealing with less-visible opportunities.

Mostly Es – Leading a business or leading the organisation. Business leadership is about organisational identity, risk-taking, creating alliances, creating competitive advantage, cross-business value creation and learning from the competition. Leading the organisation is about enterprise identity, vision and strategy, company legacy, shaping culture, creating organisational synergy, managing enterprise alliances, creating shareholder value and learning from sharing wisdom.

LEADERSHIP STYLES

Successful leadership requires self-awareness and an understanding of your own style – how you behave and the implications for others around you, both inside and outside the organisation.

THE IDEA

When to use it: When you want to improve a response or approach to a specific situation, or simply to improve the way you lead people.

Summary: Leadership is situational: you should adjust your style to match each specific challenge. For example, an approach that works well with one group of people may not work well with a different group. Deciding which approach is best involves taking into account:

- **the kind of people you're managing;**
- **the type of tasks they're completing.**

DESCRIPTION

Understanding different leadership styles

Different styles of leadership are appropriate at different times. The main styles are described below. The model of situational leadership (from Ken Blanchard and Spencer Johnson's book *The One Minute Manager*, published by Jossey Bass, 1996) is useful here.

Leadership style	Characteristics
Directing (telling) This involves structure; control and supervision; one-way communication	This approach is effective when the team is new, temporary or forming. These leaders are hands-on, decisive and involved with the needs of the task and the team. They direct the team and stress the importance of tasks and deadlines.
Coaching (engaging) This involves directing and supporting; teaching skills	This style is often preferred when the team has worked together for some time and has developed understanding and expertise. It's useful when a balance is needed between short- and long-term aspects. The leader needs to monitor the achievement of targets, but longer-term elements, such as communication networks and decision-making processes, are also important.

Leadership style	Characteristics
Supporting (developing) This involves praising, listening and facilitating development	This is suitable for a situation in which a team continues to function well. Once leaders have empowered their staff, they're no longer involved in short-term performance and operational measures. Also, the longer term is significant, with leaders focusing on individual and team development, planning and innovation.
Delegating ('hands-off' facilitation) This involves handing over responsibility for routine decisions	This is a 'hands-off' style that works best with a highly experienced, successful team. The team works well with very little involvement from the leader; instead, the leadership role is often to work externally for the team, developing networks, gaining resources, sharing best practice and expertise. Leaders may intervene in the team, if requested, to help define problems and devise solutions or to advise if a problem arises.

Using leadership styles

Success as a leader relies on using the right style at the right time. Such situational leadership draws on four management styles: directing, coaching, supporting and delegating. Adapt your approach to suit each situation.

When working with a member of your team the key question to consider is often whether to focus on the team members' *skills* (their competence) or their *attitude* (commitment). Coaching is the best approach to enhance skills, while counselling is effective for influencing behaviour, attitude and commitment. Also, remember that different styles may be needed for the same person for different parts of their job.

Each style is effective at different times. A directional approach is most appropriate when the leader needs to tell people what to do, perhaps in a crisis or when dealing with difficult personnel issues. This should be used only in exceptional circumstances. Delegating, supporting and coaching styles can be seen as a democratic approach, with the leader seeking consensus and engaging the team. This works best when you need to get your team to commit to a course of action.

Applying the right style at the right time

To know which style is appropriate to match the needs of the task or people involved, look at how people are doing in terms of their competence. This can be done by assessing their level of education, training, experience and commitment – these determine their ability, confidence and motivation. Use this information to determine which style to use. For example:

- if a person is low in confidence, this will reduce commitment, so they'll need support and praise;
- if a person is low in motivation, then listen, work out why and solve the problem (this could be lack of recognition, lack of results or lost belief in the goal).

Understand how your behaviour affects others

To improve your leadership style, it's necessary to understand the impact of your behaviour and then to adjust your style to ensure successful leadership. There are many ways to explore this, from psychometric tests to 360-degree appraisals.

The following suggestions will help you assess your approach.

- Reflect on previous situations and on things people have told you, to identify how you typically behave.
- Ask others how they view your style.
- Decide if you move easily from one style to another, as appropriate, or whether you have one dominant style.

Finally, subject your approach to specific questions. For example: Is your personal style overly formal, informal or balanced? Does it encourage and empower people? Is it prescriptive or controlling? What effect are you having on others – why might this be and how could it improve or develop?

LEADING LEADERS

If your coachees are taking on a new, senior role, it's useful to remind them of the specific challenges that come when leading people who are themselves leaders. The techniques are largely the same as for leading anyone else, with several notable additions.

THE IDEA

When to use it: When you're taking on a new role or your team is expanding – whenever you're leading leaders.

Summary: Other leaders should be granted as much freedom to lead and manage as possible – including, where feasible, the opportunity to decide what is to be implemented as well as how. Other leaders must have the freedom to decide how best to achieve what you (or the business) require of them, although it's often not possible to separate what needs to be achieved from how it will be accomplished. Although ultimate responsibility will still rest with you, this approach has the potential advantage of gaining commitment and understanding.

DESCRIPTION

What can you do to ensure your success if you're leading other people who are themselves leaders? How do you make things happen when your direct control is necessarily diluted and you can't do everything yourself? Several simple techniques will go a long way.

- **Show trust and support.** The best results are achieved when people are trusted with their responsibilities and are shown support. This requires a high level of trust and patience. Support should always be given by one leader to another in public. Not doing this can harm subordinates' confidence and their long-term ability to lead. When disagreeing with someone in private consider two interrelated questions. How will this person respond to being overruled? Is the long-term harm that will be caused by this disagreement greater or smaller than the long-term benefit that will result from having your own way?

■ **Support leaders and empower them to create change.** This means communicating a compelling vision to employees, ensuring that systems are compatible with that vision and that any obstacles to change are removed. Also, provide the training that people need – without the right skills and attitudes, people feel uncertain. Finally, confront people who undermine needed change.

■ **Consider how best to challenge and develop leaders.** A common mistake is to assume that leaders, having already achieved success, don't need challenging opportunities or professional development. Lifelong learning is an essential aspect of successful leadership and leaders should be encouraged to develop their skills. Some areas where leaders might benefit include risk-taking, developing a willingness to push out of comfort zones, self-reflection, honestly assessing successes and failures, and soliciting opinions using 360-degree appraisals to highlight areas to be reinforced.

■ **Apply the essentials of leadership** – this means being self-aware, developing empathy, adopting a positive, decisive approach, playing to people's strengths and encouraging people to learn, change, develop and improve.

We can all find ways we can fail; the leader's task is to channel people's energies so that they – and the organisation – succeed.

LOGICAL LEVELS

'Logical levels' can be used by coaches to help individuals understand what's important to people at the different levels used by human beings to make sense of their experiences.

THE IDEA

When to use it: When you want to understand or help others understand what matters to them personally, or when you want to establish a priority order for the things that matter to someone. It can also be useful for anticipating what situations could cause stress.

Summary: People will often talk about things at different 'levels'. You may hear individuals saying that on the one level they feel happy about something yet at another, they're less comfortable. Anthropologist Gregory Bateson identified basic levels of learning and change (see Michael Levin, *On Bateson's logical levels of learning theory*, Massachusetts Institute of Technology, 1975). These levels refer to the way in which we organise our experiences into a hierarchical structure.

DESCRIPTION

Understanding an individual's different logical levels

People have various ways of articulating what they need and what's important to them.

- At the *environmental level*, this can include things such as office space, lighting, desk space, cramped work areas, lack of facilities and distance from work to home.
- At the *behavioural level*, this includes the actions that are taken, what someone actually does, the things one can't do or say.

- At the *skill and ability level*, this includes the natural abilities we possess and the skills we've acquired through learning and development, or the lack of them due to insufficient training and development.
- At the *level of belief*, this includes our and others' values and opinions, the reasons we do or don't do things, and what we need to believe in to produce change or go along with the status quo.
- At the *role level*, this can include titles, job specifications, expectations and hierarchy.
- At the *identity level*, this can include things that affect us personally, what we want as a person, and things that affect who we really are.

Creating consistency and alignment between levels

We all need some sort of 'alignment' or consistency in our lives. What may be important to one person may not be to another. Whilst we may not be able to create perfect conditions for ourselves all the time, being able to have what's important most of the time contributes to our well-being.

There are a number of key questions to consider.

- What's important to you about your work at the level of the *environment*? This includes the times you work, where you work and your surroundings.
- What's important to you about your work at the level of *behaviour*? This includes the tasks you're expected to perform, the things you do and don't say, the things you're able to do, the way that you act and the way that others act towards you.
- What's important to you about your work at the level of *skills and abilities*? This includes the skills you naturally possess as well as those things you've learnt to do, plus the amount or lack of opportunity to gain more skills.
- What's important to you about your work at the level of *beliefs*? This includes such things as the beliefs your company has about its products, its passion, what it believes about its people, and the views your colleagues express about these things.

■ What's important to you about your work at the level of *identity*? This includes the possibility that you treat your job as a role and when you leave work you leave the role behind. It also includes the possibility that you are your work and take things extremely personally.

Finally, what can you do to ensure you get what's important to you? What would your first step be?

MANAGING CROSS-CULTURAL RELATIONSHIPS AND BEHAVIOUR

Globalisation has brought many benefits and opportunities, as well as risks. One of the greatest advantages is the ability to work with new people, cultures and perspectives – and several guiding principles can help ensure success.

THE IDEA

When to use it: When you're planning to work abroad or with colleagues from another culture.

Summary: Managing cross-cultural relationships involves three stages:

- **being aware of the origins, nature and influence of cultural differences and of culturally defined values and assumptions;**
- **respecting cultural differences in style and approach and ending stereotyping;**
- **reconciling cultural differences by showing people how to use the strengths of their respective values and approaches.**

DESCRIPTION
Prepare for working across cultures

This doesn't necessarily mean travelling or working abroad – it means recognising that in business, increasingly, international customers and colleagues will come to you. The following guidelines will help you to prepare for working across cultures.

Of particular significance is the need to broaden and develop your perspective. This is accomplished by recognising that:

■ your own culture is a unique peculiarity. When working across borders you will often be the 'stranger' who is perceived by others as 'strange'.

■ the culture you ignore most is your own. So, try to look at yourself from the outside: what might others think? Remember, intercultural situations offer an opportunity to reduce this blind spot – other cultures provide us with a mirror in which we can see more of our own cultural attitudes.

■ others will think and act differently to you. However, if you're convinced that your way of managing, making decisions, leading people and working generally is best, then avoid working across cultures. It will be a lot less painful for everyone – including you.

■ your behaviour needs to adapt to norms and expectations, and local customs should be respected, but this doesn't mean imitating them.

Be patient

For example, accept that your concept of time may not be shared and it can take a different amount of time than you expect to achieve results.

Beware of the 'denial of difference' and 'illusion of similarity'

For example, people may be excessively polite as a way of denying difference. Statements such as 'We share the same language...we are united by the same industry, business or values' can hide a desire to avoid confronting the reality of cultural differences. The most negative outcomes in cross-cultural collaboration occur when the people involved in a situation hold widely differing assumptions and are completely unaware that this is the case.

Denying difference matters because it means we achieve only the lowest common denominator. Denying difference can lead to superficiality, low risk-taking and avoidance of constructive confrontation.

Apply the eight preconditions for diversity in your team or business

Research suggests that eight preconditions are necessary for a business or team to benefit from identity-group differences:

- leaders must genuinely value variety of insight and opinion;
- leaders must be consistent and persevere when encouraging diversity;
- high standards of performance must be expected from everyone;
- leaders need to ensure that the working environment stimulates, encourages and supports personal development;
- leaders need to encourage openness, with a high tolerance for debate;
- the working climate (or culture) must make employees feel valued and keen to contribute;
- the vision for the team must be clear, compelling and, crucially, *practical* – informing and guiding behaviour;
- the team needs to be egalitarian and non-bureaucratic – this helps people exchange ideas and value constructive challenges to the usual way of doing things.

Take care when making jokes

Some jokes not only fail to travel across cultures, they cause offence (of course, this is true even within cultures). Humour can sometimes be a great support in cross-cultural situations but it's also one of the most culturally sensitive aspects of social life.

Understand each individual

This is accomplished by first checking your views and assumptions with others around you. Several other measures are also needed.

- Recognise that you may hold stereotypical views about other groups. Try to understand what these are and use them as prototypes to be updated or changed on the basis of experience.
- Appreciate that attribution errors occur in both directions: cultural factors can be mistakenly attributed to individuals, and vice versa.
- Understand the motives behind a specific behaviour – not superficially judging the behaviour itself nor judging it against your own cultural standards. This is particularly useful when you

come across a way of working that is strange, ineffective or meaningless.

Understand the main areas of cultural difference

Management writer Fons Trompenaars highlights the need to reconcile various cultural dilemmas.

- **Universalism versus particularism.** This cultural conflict concerns the standards by which relationships are measured. For universalists, rules and procedures are applied consistently, whereas for particularists the relationship and flexibility are more important. Universalists assume that their standards are the right standards and they attempt to change the attitudes of others to match their own. Universalist societies include Switzerland, Canada, the US and Sweden. Particularist societies are characterised by a belief that the bonds of particular relationships are stronger than abstract rules. Particularist societies include Venezuela, Korea and Russia.
- **Individualism versus communitarianism** is about the conflict between people's desires and the interests of the group to which they belong. Do people primarily regard themselves as individuals or as part of a group? In individualist cultures, people are more self-oriented than community-oriented. The individualistic culture emphasises individual freedom and responsibility. Examples of individualist societies include Israel, Canada and the US. The communitarian culture emphasises working for the interests of the group. People are mainly oriented towards common goals and objectives. The communitarian culture is notable in Egypt, Mexico, India and Japan.
- **Neutral versus affective** focuses on the extent to which people display emotions and on the interaction between reason and emotion in relationships. In neutral cultures, people are taught that it's incorrect to display emotion overtly, whereas in affective cultures, people freely express their emotions, even looking for

outlets for their feelings. Ethiopia, Japan and China are neutral cultures, whereas Spain, Egypt and Kuwait are affective.

- **Specific versus diffuse** involves the way people approach a situation as well as their degree of involvement in relationships. People from specifically oriented cultures begin by considering each element of a situation, analysing each part separately before putting them back together. The whole is the sum of its parts. Also, people from specifically oriented cultures separate their work from personal relationships. Examples include Holland, Denmark, Sweden and the UK.

  In diffusely oriented cultures, people tend to see each element as part of a bigger picture. Also, individuals engage each other across several levels at the same time; elements of life and personality are interwoven. Examples of diffuse societies include China, Nigeria and Kuwait.

- **Achievement versus ascription** focuses on how personal status is assigned. Achieved status relates to an individual's action and what you do (e.g. the US, Australia and Canada), whereas ascribed status is more concerned with who you are (e.g. Egypt, Argentina, Czech Republic).

- **Sequential versus synchronic** is about perceptions of time. People in sequential cultures tend to view time as a series of linear, passing events; they take time and schedule commitment seriously. Synchronic cultures view past, present and future as interrelated – and they usually tend to do several things at once.

- **Internal versus external control** relates to the extent to which people believe they're in control or they're affected by their environment.

People who have an internally controlled view tend to believe they can dominate their environment. This contrasts with an externally controlled view of nature, with their actions oriented towards others. They focus on their environment rather than themselves.

Reconcile differences

Resolving these cultural differences can be achieved by:

- looking for opportunities and the value with *both* perspectives, rather than favouring one or the other or seeing conflicts between different values;
- defining issues in terms of dilemmas or end results – what it is that needs to be achieved – instead of focusing on the means. Find ways to avoid compromise as this is often simply the lowest common denominator;
- reaching out to colleagues of different orientations. Their different perspectives and experiences are potentially interesting and a valuable advantage;
- being willing to invest effort communicating across cultural boundaries;
- respect and practise generic and local business customs, especially when it comes to communication.

MANAGING DIFFERENT GENERATIONS

Understanding the traits and desires of the different age groups present in the workplace allows coachees to provide them with the incentives and motivation they truly value, improving performance and morale.

THE IDEA

When to use it: When you wish to enhance your working relationship with colleagues of different generations.

Summary: It can be argued that the contemporary workplace contains four age groups.

- **Silent veterans aged 60+.**
- **Baby Boomers aged 41–58.**
- **Generation X-ers aged 24–40.**
- **Generation Y-ers aged 23 years and under.**

These different groups have different expectations and often require subtly different management techniques. With an ageing workforce and shifting demographics, the manager who can motivate regardless of people's age gains a significant advantage.

DESCRIPTION

The first priority is never discriminate on the basis of age; instead show sensitivity to the attitudes of all your employees. What one group favours may not encourage or motivate another group of people of a different age.

Next, understand the perspectives of each generation and take these into account in the way you manage.

The preferences and perspectives of different generations... (source: Harvard Management Update)	...and their implications for managers
Veterans or silents (aged 60+) tend to prefer formality, structure and hierarchy over informality. Their formative years were at a time when work was dominated by issues of structure, clarity (not ambiguity) and there was a higher degree of formality than today.	Silent veterans tend to have the most traditional ideas of interaction, favouring formal contact, face-to-face meetings and live phone calls instead of voicemail or email. Their preference for structure also means they place a high value on knowing the logic of any action or course. They typically value recognition of their skills and abilities, for example with awards and ceremonies.
Baby Boomers (aged 45–60) tend to prefer a clear series of steps towards a specific goal, and it's often useful to explain objectives and goals in people-centred terms. They are the 'hippy generation' whose formative years were the late 1960s and 1970s when social, people-centric issues increased in significance in the workplace.	When managing baby boomers, clearly define goals and break down the process into a series of individual targets. Place an emphasis on teamwork and motivational talks. Rewards should be public, with noticeable displays of recognition.
Generation X-ers (aged 28–44) expect to be told what to do but they don't like to be told how to do it. Their formative experiences took place in the 1980s and 1990s when issues of empowerment, self-determination and self-fulfilment increased in significance. This group especially dislikes jargon, platitudes, any hint of insincerity and an inability to talk straight. This may be because it obscures their ability to gather all the information they need to progress and can seem stultifying.	Allow Generation X-ers slightly more freedom to achieve their targets: tell them what to do, but allow them to decide how to achieve the goal. When managing Generation X-ers give them multiple tasks but let them set their own priorities and ways of working. Keep channels of communication open to allow ideas, opinions and feedback to be discussed. They dislike pep talks. Instead, it's often useful to provide frequent, frank feedback and to ask for their ideas and opinions. They particularly value time off and work which has meaning and is fun. Practical rewards, such as days off or monetary bonuses, are welcomed.
Generation Y-ers (sometimes also known as Nexters, aged 20–27) often display a positive, energetic approach. They value opportunities for continuous learning and building skills, they like to know their direction and they prefer informality. Their formative experiences occurred in the 2000s (e.g. through 9/11, wars in Iraq and Afghanistan, the credit crunch and economic recession). They like their work to have meaning and interest, and the idea of a career for life doesn't hold the appeal it once did.	Generation Y should be given plenty of opportunities to build their skills and experience – view yourself as both an instructive guide and a boss. Find out their personal goals and make broader company targets relevant to those individual goals. Communication should be informal and positive. Email communications work well (brief hallway encounters can also work).

MANAGING STRESS

It's important for coaches and coachees to be able to recognise the symptoms and causes of stress, as well as being able to manage their own personal stress and create conditions that detect the incidence or reduce the level of stress in others. Everyone needs a certain amount of stress or pressure – and not all stress or pressure is negative as it provides energy and motivation. However, when we go beyond our ability to deal with that level of pressure we suffer negative stress.

THE IDEA

When to use it: When an individual is suffering (or close to suffering) stress or when an individual is striving to achieve the benefits of managing stress. These include: enhanced personal effectiveness, morale and energy to achieve goals; greater efficiency and productivity; improved confidence, collaborative working and efficiency; greater innovation, boldness and an ability to manage risk.

Summary: The consequences of stress are particularly important for leaders. It reduces the leader's own personal effectiveness; it can reduce morale and sap the team's ability to achieve goals, and it can reduce overall efficiency and damage the external perception of the whole organisation. For these reasons, individuals need to manage their own stress, create conditions that reduce the level and incidence of stress in their organisation and detect the symptoms of stress in others. Most importantly, they need to have an evidence procedure that lets an individual know when they have exceeded their personal tolerance for pressure.

DESCRIPTION

An ability to manage time and stress is essential to maintain adaptability – understanding how circumstances are changing and staying flexible, positive and committed. To be adaptable and to ensure that decisions remain relevant, several techniques can be applied:

- **an awareness of stress – what it is and how to handle it;**
- **an ability to prioritise work and complete tasks swiftly and efficiently;**
- **a clear vision promoting a shared sense of purpose – this makes it easier to adapt to changing circumstances;**
- **confronting problems and their root causes early (for example, removing bureaucracy and potential frustrations);**
- **developing people's skills so they can meet the challenges of new circumstances.**

Understanding the nature of stress

Stress prevents rational, effective decisions and causes choices to be hurried, ill conceived, biased and flawed. It's much harder for people to be effective if they're stressed. More likely, they'll try to manage their way out of their stressed situation in a conventional way, concerned that an unknown approach may make things worse (ignoring the fact that conventional pressures have built up and got them to that point in the first place). Alternatively, stressed people may strike out and take a risk but, with their judgement impaired, the chance of success is limited. Finally, they may simply buckle under the pressure, trapped in a cycle of stress and tension, with potentially devastating consequences.

Recognising stress in yourself and others

It's often difficult to know when one is suffering from stress because it invariably builds up gradually over time and is all consuming and difficult to separate from normal behaviour. Also, stress is a personal matter, and the symptoms are either behavioural or physical, or both. Physical symptoms of stress include: irregular breathing, feeling tense and stiff, exhaustion, headaches, a dry mouth and throat, feeling restless or 'on edge', feeling hot, possibly with clammy hands and perspiration, sexual problems, loss of appetite or weight gain, and addiction (to drugs, alcohol or nicotine).

These problems can occur at different times for reasons quite unrelated to stress; however, they may be stress-related if several occur at the same time, if they appear constantly or if they appear with no apparent cause. The behavioural symptoms of stress are no less significant or serious and include feeling worried, demotivated, irritated, withdrawn, upset, exhausted or weary, angry, misunderstood, frustrated and powerless.

These symptoms lead to difficulties in concentrating, focusing, being creative, making decisions or solving problems – in short, judgement is impaired. There's also a self-reinforcing 'downward cycle' of stress: many of the symptoms, such as anger or inefficiency, prevent the problem being solved, and more than that they actually exacerbate the situation and cause greater stress leading to more problems and greater stress.

Managing the causes of stress

What typically causes stress? There are many careers and situations recognised as being highly stressful but the truth is that anyone, at any level, in any job, can suffer stress. The causes and symptoms of stress are similar and some examples include:

- **work overload and an increase in out-of-hours working;**
- **absenteeism due to ill health;**
- **high employee turnover;**
- **reduced job satisfaction;**
- **breakdown in communication;**
- **a focus on unproductive tasks.**

However, any number of factors may contribute to poor performance. In fact, common causes of stress at work can be broken down into five areas.

- **Factors that are an integral part of the job.**
- **Factors that relate to the nature of position and to what the person actually does.**
- **Relationships which are difficult to manage, largely because of the way that people think and behave.**

- Change is another source of stress as people are wary of change.
- Life causes of stress such as the death of someone close, divorce, separation from a partner or moving house. Interestingly, happy times can also cause worry and stress, notably weddings, pregnancy and holidays.

Stress is therefore complex and rarely caused by a single factor. In fact, it is not only the range of issues that cause stress but the nature of the individual experiencing it and how they react.

Techniques for minimising stress

- **Know yourself** and consider what *you* would recognise as symptoms of stress. To help, think about previous times that were stressful for you and remember how you felt, how you behaved, what the result was and whether, with the benefit of hindsight, you handled it in the best way possible.
- **Take responsibility** – avoid denying the problem or blaming someone (or something) else. Even if it's someone else's fault, it's you who's being affected and you who must resolve the underlying problem.
- **Consider what's causing stress.** Is it resulting from the job, your role, work relationships, change or something else – perhaps not work related at all?
- **Anticipate stressful periods and plan for them.** Consider what may have worked in the past, what you did and how successful it was. Also, consider how to remove or reduce the cause of stress, or learn to accept it if it can't be removed.
- **Use simple management techniques.** For example, time management and assertiveness are two of the most important skills as many difficulties are caused either by time pressures or relationship issues that could be prevented by more assertive, controlled behaviour. Communication, decision making and problem solving have much to offer once the problem has been acknowledged and the sources of stress identified.

■ **Understand that you need to work at relaxing.** This may mean finding an activity or interest that suits you best and then absorbing yourself in it. Time away from the causes of stress can help to put the situation in perspective and lead to a new approach that provides a solution.

MENTORING

Mentoring has much in common with coaching – both are about supporting individuals to overcome problems, achieve success and realise their full potential. Mentoring specifically involves offering guidance, advice and support to increase the understanding and effectiveness of another person.

THE IDEA

When to use it: When an individual would benefit from practical or directive support.

Summary: Mentoring takes a longer-term view and is more advisory than coaching. It typically provides an individual with:

- **the advice, guidance and support of a trusted adviser;**
- **a 'big picture' view, clear of routine concerns;**
- **a sounding board for the exploration of ideas;**
- **perceptions that are more objective and detached than those of a line manager;**
- **access to a network;**
- **the benefit of another person's personal experience.**

DESCRIPTION
Developing your mentoring skills

Relevant work experience is a vital element for successful mentoring. This doesn't mean that mentors need necessarily be tutors, nor does it require mentors to be experts in a particular topic. However, mentors do need to have an understanding of what the learner is trying to achieve. Several skills and principles are especially significant.

- **Management perspective, meaning that mentors understand management practice, pressures and techniques (for example,** delegation, team-building, time management and problem-solving – among others).

■ **Credibility and 'organisational know-how'** are important as mentors need to enjoy personal and professional credibility within the organisation in order to get things done and support their learner, and they need to understand the system in which the learner works.

■ **Accessibility** – meaning that mentors are available to their learners when the need arises.

■ **Communication and interpersonal skills** – mentors need to be able to get the best out of their learners, building trust and helping them to develop their full potential. Mentors also need to be sensitive and able to understand the learners' ideas, views and feelings. Of all the interpersonal skills, the core skills needed here are questioning and active listening.

■ **An empowering approach** that has clear belief in the abilities of their learners is necessary from mentors. They need to be able to create the conditions for the learners to grow, to try out new skills and methods and to make a greater contribution to the organisation.

■ **Creativity and innovation** – mentors must be open to new ideas, and be inventive and able to consider (and even to suggest) new ways of doing things or approaching problems or issues. Mentors ideally need to be able to perceive different and useful connections and patterns and to be creative problem-solvers in their own right.

■ **A focus on personal development** is an important quality for mentors; they should have experience of, and support for, the development of others.

Avoiding problems with mentoring

The qualities of a poor mentor or coach are the same. They include dominating and prescribing solutions; being critical or inflexible; being insensitive and authoritarian – for example, imposing solutions, plans and arbitrary deadlines; rigidly defending the status quo, and above all, talking, not listening.

These pitfalls can often result from insecurity. Also, some of these attitudes may result from a fear of change, and this, too, is nothing to be worried about. The answer is to focus on the needs of the task and the individual – what will it take to get the job done? Remember, change and innovation are the only ways to make progress.

THE META-MIRROR

How can you help people to alter or adjust their outlook and perceptions? One of the best ways is to use the meta-mirror, a technique that literally encourages individuals to see things from a different point of view, and to prepare and rehearse a conversation.

THE IDEA

When to use it: When a discussion needs to be rehearsed or, more generally, when greater empathy and understanding of someone else's position is needed

Summary: The meta-mirror is a way to help people see things from another perspective – someone else's point of view. It is especially valuable when preparing for an important conversation or discussion, or to develop a relationship. It can be used anywhere, at any time.

DESCRIPTION

There are several simple, sequential steps to follow when using the meta-mirror. (For the purposes of this exercise, to keep the explanation simple, we're assuming here that the coachee is female and the person she has an issue with is a male colleague.)

1 **The coachee needs to have a relationship issue that she would like to resolve in a conversation.**
2 **Establish whether this conversation will take place seated or standing, and in what environment – for example, will it be in an office, a boardroom or somewhere else?**
3 **If the conversation is likely to be held seated, place two chairs opposite each other and invite the coachee to sit down. Then say to her: 'Imagine that your colleague is sitting in front of you now, in that chair, and say whatever you want to him'. This is called the first position.**

4 Once she's finished speaking, ask the coachee to stand and check that she's ready to continue.

5 Now ask her to sit in the other chair (that her imaginary colleague was sitting in) and, crucially, *adopt his physiological aspects.* Encourage the coachee to replicate her colleague's physiology by asking if he would sit upright, hold his head to one side, frown, lean back, cross his legs, put his hands behind his head and so on.

6 Once you're comfortable that she's done this, ask the coachee to put herself into her imaginary colleague's shoes and accept and respond to the information she's given him. Observe what takes place. This is the second position. Once this is finished, ask her to stand and shake herself a little to return to normal.

7 Take the coachee to a different part of the room where you can both observe the two chairs. Alternatively, bring a third chair into play and ask the coachee to sit here. Ask her to imagine her observations about what's going on between these two people. For example, try asking 'what resources do you need to handle this more effectively?' Be aware that whatever she comes up with reflects her thoughts and feelings and is valid. But words like 'compassion', 'confidence' and 'clarity' are the sorts of things people say. This is the third position.

8 Go back to the two chairs and say: 'Having heard what was said by yourself and by your colleague, and seeing what you've just told me from the third position, now sit down again as yourself in the first chair and say whatever you have to say to your colleague.'

Observe and discuss the differences in the manner, content and delivery of her message with the new information gained from the changes in perceptual positions.

MIRACLE QUESTION

There's invariably one question that can help liberate the way individuals think – the trick is to find it, or, better still, help them to find it. A typical miracle question can often simply begin 'What if...?'

THE IDEA

When to use it: The miracle question works best when individuals are stuck, perhaps unable to identify their goal, think creatively or generate options. It can also be used to improve the overall quality of thinking in these areas.

Summary: The miracle question can take a number of forms, such as: 'If, overnight a miracle happens and, when you wake up, things are exactly as you want them to be – what will they be like?'

The right question can help people learn, build confidence, increase understanding, awareness and insight, and also help them to make progress. The miracle question goes even further: it helps an individual cut through confusion, indecision or trepidation. The miracle question's main benefit and purpose is to enable the coachee to provide his or her own solution.

DESCRIPTION

Helping coachees to find the miracle question, the notion that will help unblock or stimulate their thinking, is a very useful skill for a coach to have. Several simple techniques can help but it's useful for coaches to keep one thing constantly at the back of their mind when helping individuals through a difficult or challenging situation: what's the miracle question for them, now?

- **Ask the coachees for their miracle question. What's the thing they want to know most?**
- **Ask them for their ideal situation. Be persistent and use probing questions to help them achieve a breakthrough in their thinking.**

■ **Miracle questions can often begin with a standard root; use the following standard roots and adapt them to the specific challenge being faced.**

   ■ 'What is stopping you from...?'
   ■ 'How could you...?'
   ■ 'If you could wave a magic wand, what would you do?' (Follow this up with an exploration of *why*, or how elements of this approach could realistically be adapted to the situation.)
   ■ 'If you had a time machine that could take you to a point in the future where everything you hope for has been achieved, what's it like?'

THE MYERS-BRIGGS TYPE INDICATOR (MBTI)

The Myers-Briggs type indicator (MBTI) assessment is one of the world's most popular and widely used psychometric tests. Its value lies in helping people understand how they (and others) perceive the world and make decisions.

THE IDEA

When to use it: When you want to reflect on, and explore differences in thinking preferences between people.

Summary: The Myers-Briggs type indicator (MBTI) assessment is a psychometric test that assesses psychological preferences in the way that people perceive the world and make decisions. Developed by Katharine Cook Briggs and her daughter, Isabel Briggs Myers, during World War II, the initial questionnaire became the world-renowned Myers-Briggs type indicator.

Central to the MBTI is the theory of *psychological type*, originally developed by Carl Jung. With MBTI, there are four pairs of personality preferences (also known as dichotomies):

- **extraversion or introversion;**
- **sensing or intuition;**
- **thinking or feeling;**
- **judging or perceiving.**

The Myers-Briggs approach views personality type as preferred ways of thinking and acting that an individual is either born with or develops. The MBTI sorts these psychological differences into four opposite pairs, so consequently there 16 possible psychological types. Crucially,

continued overleaf

> continued
>
> none of these types is 'better' or 'worse' than the other, just preferred by individuals depending on their personality. This is similar to people preferring to write with their left hand; they may be able to write with the other hand at some point in their life, but it's harder and less natural for them. The value of the MBTI lies in its ability to explain the thinking preferences of individuals – such as how they search for information and how they prefer to process information to make decisions.

DESCRIPTION

Attitudes: extraversion and introversion

People who prefer extraversion draw energy from action. They tend to act, then reflect, then act again. If they're inactive their level of energy and motivation tends to decline. Conversely, people who prefer introversion become less energised as they act: they prefer to reflect, then act, then reflect again. People who prefer introversion need time out to reflect in order to rebuild energy. Also, the extravert's flow is directed outward toward people and objects, and the introvert's is directed inward toward concepts and ideas.

As a result, extraverts are action-oriented and desire breadth, while introverts are thought-oriented and seek depth. Extraverts often prefer more frequent interaction, while introverts prefer more substantial interaction.

Functions: Sensing (S) and iNtuition (N) and Thinking (T)/Feeling (F)

Jung identified two pairs of psychological functions:

- **two perceiving functions, sensing and intuition;**
- **two judging functions, thinking and feeling.**

In the view of the MBTI, each person uses one of these four functions more dominantly and proficiently than the other three; however, all four functions are used at different times depending on the circumstances.

Sensing and intuition are the information-gathering (perceiving) functions. They describe how new information is understood and interpreted.

■ Individuals who prefer *sensing* are more likely to trust information that is in the present and tangible (i.e. information that can be understood by the five senses). They tend to distrust hunches that seem to come out of nowhere. They prefer to look for details and facts. For them, the meaning is in the data.

■ In contrast, people who prefer *intuition* tend to trust information that is more abstract or theoretical and can be associated with other information. They may be more interested in future possibilities. They tend to trust flashes of insight from the unconscious mind. The meaning is in how the data relates to the pattern or theory.

Thinking and feeling are the decision-making (judging) functions. The thinking and feeling functions are both used to make rational decisions based on the data received from their information-gathering functions (sensing or intuition).

■ People who prefer *thinking* tend to decide things from a more detached standpoint, measuring the decision by what seems reasonable, logical, causal and consistent, matching a given set of rules.

■ People who prefer *feeling* tend to come to decisions by associating or empathising with the situation, looking at it 'from the inside' and weighing up the situation so they can decide how to achieve, on balance, the greatest harmony, consensus and fit, considering the needs of the people involved.

However, people who prefer thinking don't necessarily 'think better' than their 'feeling' counterparts; the opposite preference is an equally rational way of coming to decisions. Also, the MBTI assessment is a measure of preference, not ability. Similarly, those who prefer feeling don't necessarily have 'better' emotional reactions than their thinking counterparts.

Dominance

Although people use all four cognitive functions (sensing, intuition, thinking and feeling), one function is generally used in a more conscious and confident way. This dominant function is supported by the secondary (auxiliary) function and, to a lesser degree, the tertiary function. The fourth and least conscious function is always the opposite of the dominant function.

The four functions operate in conjunction with the attitudes (extraversion and introversion). Each function is used in either an extraverted or introverted way. A person whose dominant function is extraverted intuition, for example, uses intuition very differently from someone whose dominant function is introverted intuition.

Lifestyle: judgement (J) and perception (P)

Myers and Briggs added another dimension to Jung's typological model by showing that people also have a preference for either *judging* (thinking or feeling) or *perceiving* (sensing or intuition) when relating to the outside world (extraversion).

People with a preference for *judging* (J) show the world their preferred judging function (thinking or feeling). So, TJ (thinking/judging) types tend to appear as logical, and FJ (feeling/judging) types are empathetic. Judging types prefer certainty and like to have matters settled.

Types with a preference for *perception* (P) show the world their preferred perceiving function (sensing or intuition). So, SP (sensing/perceiving) types tend to appear to the world as concrete and NP (intuition/perceiving) types as abstract. Perceiving types prefer to keep decisions open and flexible.

PRIORITISING AND MANAGING YOUR TIME

Managing time is about understanding and managing *priorities* – what you want to achieve – as well as your ability to do this efficiently, in the way you envisage. Several practical techniques can help.

THE IDEA

When to use it: When time pressures are leading to inefficiency or stress, or to enhance personal effectiveness and productivity.

Summary: Time management is an entirely personal activity, yet often individuals expect their time to be managed by others and they'll assume that their manager understands their priorities and workload. The starting place for efficient time management is the fundamental principle that every person – at every level in the organisation – needs to develop a personal sense of time. This means:

- *taking responsibility* for managing your time and setting goals and priorities;
- using all of your time to the greatest effect and *planning* your use of time;
- taking action to ensure that manageable pressure doesn't become intolerable stress because of problems with time.

DESCRIPTION
Planning your use of time

To succeed, planning needs to be done regularly and routinely; it's not just about listing tasks but analysing and prioritising them, too. There are three levels of planning.

1 **Identifying long-term goals.** This means understanding what you want to achieve in the next year and beyond, what goals you want to complete and, perhaps most importantly, what skills you need to develop.

2 **Making medium-term plans.** These cover anything from the next few days to the next three months, depending on the environment and situation. For instance, in some industries a few days may be critical, requiring detailed planning, whereas for others a longer time-frame is helpful to set goals and priorities.

3 **Planning the day.** It's easy for time to pass on unproductive tasks. The best approach is to decide what needs to be accomplished that day, how long it will take and when the task will start and finish. Analyse each task and ask:

- Is it really necessary?
- Is it better done (or more appropriately done) by someone else?
- Can it reasonably be delegated?
- What is the appropriate quality standard required for this work?
- How urgent is it relative to the other tasks for today? One technique here is to prioritise work on a scale of A, B and C, where A is the most important task(s); B tasks are important but not as important as A, while C tasks are those that are desirable to complete but can wait if necessary.

Organising and efficiently managing your work

Using committed time, such as travelling, is useful, together with identifying and removing time-stealers such as unnecessary meetings. Best practice includes organising work, managing meetings and delegating.

Using skills of assertion

Time pressures can frequently result from people being 'put upon' or asked to do work they feel they cannot refuse. The antidote to this is assertion and includes several techniques (which of these could be improved?):

- **communicating your feelings and priorities clearly, firmly and politely;**

- understanding that you can say no – or not at the moment;
- getting the ground rules right with employees, suppliers, customers and colleagues. For example, avoid getting into a routine where you're expected to be the one who takes on the extra work;
- ensuring that the job description is both fair and appropriate, taking steps to change it if necessary;
- not being afraid to ask for help when you need it.

PROBLEM SOLVING

Everyone encounters problems at some point; what matters is helping coachees understand their causes, find and put the best solution into practice – and learn the lessons.

THE IDEA

When to use it:	Whenever an issue, obstacle or problem needs resolving.
Summary:	The need to solve problems arises throughout organisations and life. Problem solving involves a logical and systematic approach to defining the problem, generating solutions and then choosing and implementing the best option. However, there are difficulties and hidden traps within problem-solving, such as the danger of over-analysis. Often, what's really required is nothing more than a period of thought and discussion.

Common sense is a large part of problem solving but two factors also need to be considered: the decision-maker's personal style as well, as the need to test and perfect solutions.

Commitment to a particular solution also involves the emotions, sense of self and personal values. No matter how logical, can the coachee commit to carrying it out? This is worth a final check before the action plan is drawn up!

DESCRIPTION

Problem solving has several broad phases. It can help to decide:

■ **the area of greatest relevance for your particular situation;**
■ **where (and how) your problem-solving skills could improve.**

Identifying and understanding problems

How can the causes of a problem – and the likely effectiveness of a solution – be clearly recognised? Some of the most popular methods include:

- **using cause and effect analysis.** By deepening your understanding of the problem, you're better able logically to extrapolate a solution. Do this by identifying the root causes of the problem and collecting data on the causes of the problem. Asking the staff involved their opinions should help pin down the cause or causes, which can then be dealt with.
- **applying Pareto analysis.** Frequently recurring problems may, in fact, be several completely different problems all linked to each other and with many causes. Pareto analysis organises data so that the most significant factors are clear. This method is based upon the 80-20 Pareto principle: that 80 per cent of problems are caused by 20 per cent of possible factors. Tackling a problem requires a focus on the troublesome 20 per cent.

The four steps in Pareto analysis are:

1 identifying the overarching problem;
2 determining the causal factors and how often they occur;
3 listing the biggest factors – Pareto analysis applies when few factors are involved;
4 developing a solution targeting each factor individually.

This approach has the potential to eliminate the biggest causes of a problem, which often prevents it recurring or, at the very least, mitigates its effects. But, it's less useful when a large number of factors are more or less equally responsible, as it's difficult and time consuming to treat each one and pointless to prioritise the order that they're dealt with. However, the more complicated the problem, the less likely it is that Pareto analysis will help to find a solution.

- **Using Kepner-Tregoe (KT) analysis** to find out why something that should work is failing and then fix it. Its emphasis on solid, rational analysis makes it suited to 'hard', rather than 'soft', management issues. For example, it's used to explain deviations from the norm, quality or process problems.

Applying KT analysis is simple and methodical. It starts by specifying the problem in detail, often by answering several key questions.

- *What* is the problem or deviation?
- *Where* does it occur?
- *When* does it (or did it) occur?
- *How* does it occur? Specifically, *how often* does it happen and *how old* is the process when it first occurs?
- *How big* is the problem (how much is affected in real terms or as a proportion of the whole)?

By observing the situation and answering these questions, it's possible to define what the problem is – as well as what the problem *is not*. Using this information, the next stage is to examine the differences between what should happen and what does happen – preparing a list of possible causes either for each problem in turn or, if they're linked in a process, for the problem as a whole.

Generating creative options, ideas and solutions

Which technique is best? There are many ways to generate problem-solving ideas – some of the most popular are described below (for further ideas see 'Developing creativity and innovation').

- **Creative problem-solving techniques when time is short.**
  These include:
  - trying first (and asking for forgiveness later!);
  - test marketing;
  - ensuring that teams are as varied and diverse as possible;
  - seeking external input;
  - reducing – and virtually eliminating – hierarchy;
  - involving people, generating a sense of play and working without; boundaries
  - being flexible about working arrangements;
  - accepting that it's all right to try and fail;
  - imposing a deadline, while allowing some time for people to be creative.

- **Heuristics:** using experience to guide future plans and decisions.
- **Mind mapping:** organising thoughts and ideas into a clear form from which patterns and new approaches emerge or crystallise.
- **Lateral thinking,** combining ideas and concepts that haven't previously been brought together. Also, lateral thinking removes binding assumptions by asking *what if*? questions.
- **Questioning** and challenging the way that alternatives are generated. This must happen in a supportive environment and is the essential first step in breaking traditional thinking. It often helps to question established logic, asking *why*? As well as *why not*?
  - *Brainstorming* so that new ideas are generated, discussed, developed and prioritised. When it comes to brainstorming, the rules are: quantity matters, suspend judgement, freewheel and encourage every idea, cross-fertilise ideas, don't rush to judgement and plan implementation.

Making and implementing the decision

Select the most promising solution and plan its implementation. Common dangers at this point include:

- procrastination and decision avoidance. This usually results in a loss of control;
- paralysis by analysis. Over-analysing a situation can result in delay and has the same effect as procrastination;
- not managing (or mismanaging) risk. The risk in a solution needs to be carefully assessed. Think about the worst that could happen, assessing where the weaknesses lie, and how this risk could be minimised (for example, is additional support required or is a fallback position needed?);
- disregarding intuition and experience. You need to be able to trust your own judgement. Be prepared to rely on nothing more than intuition and experience;
- lacking confidence or conviction. Confidence in the solution is essential; a half-hearted approach is risky at best.

QUESTIONING

Non-directive coaching relies on the ability to question – it's an essential skill and the essence of coaching.

THE IDEA

When to use it: Always – this isn't so much a coaching technique, *it is coaching.*

Summary: The main objective of a coach is to help the coachees improve their position by learning, achieving a goal, making a decision, resolving an issue or simply improving their understanding – all by using effective questioning rather than by simply presenting a solution or the coach's viewpoint. This is because questioning is much more likely to produce a result for individuals once they've focused on the issues and considered their own solutions.

DESCRIPTION

Some of the most useful or typical questions to use during a coaching conversation include the following (note that these questions be used as part of the GROW process).

- What are you trying to achieve?
- How will you know when you've achieved it?
- Would you define it as an end goal or a performance goal?
- If it's an end goal, what performance goal could be related to it?
- Is the goal specific and measurable?
- To what extent can you control the result? What sort of things won't you have control over?
- Do you feel that achieving the goal will stretch or break you?
- When do you want to achieve the goal by?
- What are the milestones or key points on the way to achieving your goal?
- Who's involved and what effect could they have on the situation?

- What have you done about this situation so far, and what were the results?
- What are the major constraints in finding a way forward?
- Are these constraints major or minor? How could their effect be reduced?
- What other issues are occurring at work that might have a bearing on your goal?
- What options do you have?
- If you had unlimited resources, what options would you have?
- Could you link your goal to some other organisational issue?
- What would be the perfect solution?

REFRAMING

Reframing is a technique widely used in neuro linguistic programming (NLP) that allows individuals to see the world in a different way. It is based on the principle that behaviour can be useful or not in any given context. Some of the behaviours we are proud of and are useful when used appropriately; they are not useful when used in the wrong context. Conversely, our negative behaviours can be useful within certain contexts. Reframing is when a behaviour is presented in a new way so as to change the coachees' perception of the meanings of the behaviour. By changing the way that the behaviour is perceived, it gives the person the choice of using it in a particular context or not.

THE IDEA

When to use it: When we need more options or when our current normal behaviour is not working for us.

Summary: Reframing occurs when another meaning or another sense is assigned by finding a new and different way to describe a situation or context. This means someone can come to see a situation in another frame. A frame refers to a belief that limits our view of the world. If we remove this limiting belief, then new ideas, interpretations and possibilities can develop.

DESCRIPTION

Reframing is based on the view that if we see something in one particular way then our actions respond accordingly. So, for example, if we view something as being threatening then we respond defensively. However, if we change our frame of reference by looking at the same situation from a different point of view, we can change and improve the way we respond.

Context reframing

This type of reframing is based on the view that the *meaning* of a particular behaviour or event is tied to the *context* in which it occurs. Fundamentally, every action or behaviour is appropriate in some context. With a context reframe, a person takes the disliked behaviour and asks: 'Where or when could this behaviour be useful?' or: 'In what other context would this particular behaviour be of value?'

For example, one individual's work used to be a little slower than that of her colleagues. She felt pressured and feared that this was what her boss focused on. After a little while, however, her mentor pointed out that the quality of her work was superb – valued by customers and a standard for everyone else. The individual wasn't slow or unproductive; she was meticulous and thorough. This subsequently had implications for the way everyone worked and the way the office was organised. From then on, the individual met with clients and set the standard internally precisely because she was so expert.

A *context reframe* leaves the meaning of a situation or behaviour the same and shows how it could be a useful response in a different context.

Reframing questions

■ **For coachees who overuse a 'positive' characteristic or behaviour – for example, a good sense of humour – get them to ask themselves: 'When could having a good sense of humour not be helpful?' The answer may relate to when they're trying to be taken seriously or empathise with someone in distress.**

For coachees obsessively worrying about a negative aspect of their behaviour – for example, 'I'm a pessimist' – ask: 'When could being a pessimist be really helpful?' The answer may be when a job has a high element of risk or importance.

SCENARIO THINKING

Scenarios don't predict the future but they do illuminate the causes of change. This, in turn, helps managers to take greater control when conditions shift. Scenarios help managers tackle risk, uncertainty and complexity. By contemplating a range of possible futures, issues are better understood and decisions are better informed and more likely to succeed.

THE IDEA

When to use it: When coachees need to develop or implement a business strategy.

Summary: Scenario planning enables organisations to rehearse the future, to walk the battlefield before battle commences so that they're better prepared. Their value lies not in a prediction of the future, but in their ability to recognise and understand future developments, enabling managers to influence events. The benefits of scenario planning include:

- greater understanding of the present and the way that the world is changing;
- the ability to challenge established views, overcome complacency and halt the 'tyranny of the present' which leads us to overlook threats and opportunities;
- the opportunity to test new ideas as well as established strategies;
- greater ownership of ideas and decisions;
- stimulating creativity and innovation by considering different possible futures and opening minds to new possibilities;
- improved insight and learning, helping people to understand their environment, consider the future, share knowledge and assess strategic options;
- generating teamwork and helping to create a shared view.

DESCRIPTION
Understand how scenario thinking works
There are several important points to remember about scenarios including:

- scenario planning works best when it involves people at all levels of the organisation;
- critically assessing each scenario keeps the process focused, relevant and valuable;
- don't try to predict the future; instead, try to understand the forces that will shape it;
- encourage creative thinking, and don't allow existing biases to guide the process. Also, ensure that the process isn't overshadowed by operational pressures, as these can limit energy and creativity;
- understand the insights, the reasons why things are happening a certain way, and relate them to the organisation's future.

Follow the scenario planning process
Steps in using the scenario process include:

- planning and structuring the scenario process;
- exploring the context in which the future will develop;
- developing the scenarios (assessing the influences that are shaping the future);
- analysing the scenarios;
- using the scenarios.

Planning and structuring the scenario process. The first stage is to create a team to plan and structure the process.

Exploring the scenarios. Now discuss the context forces that are shaping the future.

Developing the scenarios. The next stage is to identify the forces that'll have an impact over an agreed period. Select three possible outcomes and list the forces that could lead to each of them. This will help show how these forces link together and will help you to write 'the story of the future'.

Analysing the scenarios. The analysis stage examines external issues and internal logic. What are the priorities and concerns? How likely is each scenario? Why might it occur, why might it fail to emerge? At this point, it's helpful to remember that the aim isn't to pinpoint future events; rather it's to consider the forces which may push the future along different paths.

Using the scenarios. Working backwards from the future to the present, formulate an action plan so that when the scenario events occur they'll be recognised and responded to quickly and effectively.

SETTING OBJECTIVES AND SMART GOALS

When setting goals, using the SMART approach will ensure that your coachees have goals that are appropriate, achievable and successful.

THE IDEA

When to use it: Whenever you need to focus someone on a specific objective or series of objectives, for example, at an annual appraisal, when someone starts a new role, or simply at the start of a new project.

Summary: Objectives and goals should be SMART: **s**pecific, **m**easurable, **a**chievable, **r**elevant, and **t**ime-constrained.

DESCRIPTION
Developing a SMART action plan

Think about a current goal you have or one you want to address in the future. Answer the following questions to assess the robustness of your approach to goal-setting, monitoring and achievement. Also, comment on how you could improve your approach.

- **What is your goal?**
- **Is it specific? What, exactly, will success look like? Is it an end goal or a performance goal?**
- **Is it measurable? How will progress be measured and monitored?**
- **Is it achievable? Do you have the skills and resources needed? How will you succeed and what will you do? What could go wrong? What are the risks?**
- **Is it relevant? How does it relate to other people and activities? Are these links understood and could this goal benefit from other activities or expertise elsewhere in the organisation?**

■ **What is the timescale? Are there milestones or dependencies in the plan?**

Setting objectives

Objectives should be reviewed and adjusted regularly to reflect strategic and individual changes (e.g. role changes and development needs). When setting objectives, it can help to discuss, agree and document expectations for what will be achieved and how it will be accomplished. It can also help to set objectives in a balanced scorecard format, grouped into these key elements:

■ **people**
■ **customers**
■ **financial**
■ **process**

In addition:

■ **a line manager should reflect the objectives set by their own manager;**
■ **individuals should prepare objectives for their personal development – these could be based on development opportunities identified previously;**
■ **the employee and line manager should discuss the expectations and priorities for the role;**
■ **a series of SMART objectives should then be agreed.**

Another model of goal-setting is the well-formed outcomes model (see 'well-formed outcomes' on p.260), found in many neuro linguistic programming (NLP) techniques.

SIX THINKING HATS

'Six thinking hats' is a powerful technique created by Edward de Bono (see Edward de Bono's *Six Thinking Hats* – the most recent edition is published by Penguin, 2002). It's used to look at decisions from a number of perspectives, forcing coachees to think differently and acquire a rounded view of a situation.

THE IDEA

When to use it: To improve decision making, problem solving, innovation and creativity, and to increase confidence and flexibility when faced with new or challenging situations.

Summary: Many successful people think from a rational, positive viewpoint. However, if they don't look at a problem from an emotional, creative or negative viewpoint, they can underestimate resistance to plans, fail to make creative leaps and overlook the importance of contingency plans. Conversely, pessimists can be excessively defensive, while emotional people can fail to look at decisions calmly and rationally. Each of these positions or 'thinking hats' is a different style of thinking, and the 'six thinking hats' technique will help you assess problems from many angles, enabling you to make decisions that combine ambition, effectiveness, sensitivity and creativity.

DESCRIPTION

Adopt a different hat based on your specific situation and priorities at a particular time.

■ **White hat. Focus on the data available. Look at the information you have and see what you can learn from it. Look for gaps in your knowledge and either try to fill them or take account of them, by analysing past trends and data.**

- **Red hat.** Look at problems using intuition, gut reaction and emotion. Try to think how other people will react emotionally and try to understand the responses of people who don't know your reasoning.
- **Black hat.** Look at all the bad points of the issue, trying to see why it might not work. This highlights the weak points in a plan, allowing you to eliminate or alter them or to prepare contingency plans for them. This helps to make plans more resilient. It's one of the real benefits of this technique, as problems can be anticipated and countered.
- **Yellow hat.** This requires positive thinking and optimism, helping you to see the benefits of the decision. It'll help you to keep going when everything looks difficult.
- **Green hat.** This involves developing creative solutions. It's a freewheeling way of thinking, in which there's little criticism of ideas.
- **Blue hat.** This emphasises process control and is exhibited by people chairing meetings. When ideas are running dry, it can be useful to use green hat thinking, as the creative approach can stimulate fresh ideas.

SUCCEEDING IN A NEW JOB

Moving into a new role is always challenging, but if your coachees take swift, early action in several areas, it will help them to succeed.

THE IDEA

When to use it: When you're starting a new role.

Summary: Moving into a new role is always challenging but taking practical action in several areas will help you to succeed. It's valuable to:

- **establish credibility and promote yourself;**
- **understand the challenge;**
- **accelerate your learning and get oriented;**
- **match your approach to the situation;**
- **secure early wins;**
- **agree success and negotiate resources;**
- **build your team;**
- **communicate your vision;**
- **manage yourself.**

DESCRIPTION
Establish credibility and promote yourself

This means achieving the right balance between being modest and being a self-publicist. Promoting yourself does not mean boasting about your achievements but it does mean establishing your credibility, being clear about why you're the best candidate and reassuring those around you that you'll enable the business to succeed. To do this, prepare yourself mentally for the new role by understanding what you have to offer, what you've achieved and why you're the best appointment.

Mental preparation also means taking a step back and considering what skills are required. One of the biggest pitfalls is assuming that what's made you successful in the past will ensure success in the future – it won't. Experience is valuable but you also need to focus on the specific, individual needs of the new role. Also, when starting a new senior role you need to be yourself and understand your leadership style. Although there are no hard and fast rules, leaders tend to be more credible when they're:

■ demanding but realistic, accessible but not overly familiar;
■ decisive, thoughtful, focused and flexible;
■ active and energetic but not distracting or disruptive;
■ willing to make tough decisions but focused on fairness and people.

Understand the challenge

Even the best-prepared leaders are unable to know everything they need to function effectively in a new role; you'll need to climb the learning curve quickly – after all, expectations are high when a new leader arrives and it's an excellent opportunity to make progress. Unfortunately, the pressure of time increases the likelihood that something will be missed. To understand the challenge of the new role swiftly and thoroughly, you should do the following.

■ **Establish new working relationships and build trust** – while this takes time, it also takes attention and effort.
■ **Master technical issues** – talking to people is essential, not just employees at all levels but also customers and suppliers – what are their perceptions and aspirations?
■ **Be sensitive to political and cultural issues** – get an understanding of the informal processes and alliances that exist.
■ **Manage expectations** – carefully deflating those views that are unrealistically high while taking advantage of those that are useful.
■ **Maintain your equilibrium and set the right pace.** It's easy to get carried away, either trying to do too much or else moving too cautiously. You need to find a pace that's good for the business and sustainable for you.

Accelerate your learning and get oriented

You need to get to know your new organisation quickly, and this means understanding its markets, customers, products, systems and structures, as well as the people, culture (the way things are done) and politics. Several techniques can help.

■ Categorising formal information into A, B and C. Information in category A is vital, valuable or time-sensitive. B is very useful now or it will be in the future. C is either useful background information or material that can wait.
■ Focus on the information that you need to know.
■ Using informal sources of information.

Match your approach to the situation

Professor Michael Watkins of Harvard Business School identifies four types of business situation that new leaders must contend with: start-up, turnaround, realignment and sustaining success. Each of these situations has its own specific challenges.

■ Start-up is characterised by the need to assemble the capabilities required to launch and develop a new business.
■ Turnaround involves taking a business that's struggling, stabilising it and getting it back on track.
   As with start-up, this situation is resource-intensive and requires determination and a capacity to make tough decisions quickly – ruthless prioritisation is particularly important.
■ Realignment means revitalising a business or team that's drifting, showing signs of concern or operating on a plateau rather than improving. The challenges are to deal with deeply ingrained and possibly outdated attitudes that no longer contribute to performance, to convince employees of the need for change and to refocus the organisation (probably by restructuring the top team).
■ Sustaining success is no less challenging. The task is to preserve and build on the best features of a team or business and take it to the next level. This means avoiding decisions that cause problems and finding ways to innovate and do even better. Invariably the foundations for sustained success are already

present and a strong team is already in place, but this success can also mean that people are wedded to the current business formula without seeing the need for it to evolve. Changing these attitudes is particularly challenging if a revered leader has created the top team and you're seen as an out-of-touch newcomer. The solution is to recognise success, involve people in new developments and challenge them to go even further.

Secure early wins

Achieving early wins is important – they energise people and build momentum, they establish your credibility, they either show that there's still room for improvement or highlight how things could be done better (and they're beneficial in their own right). Early wins don't need to be big but they do need to be significant and quick.

Agree success and negotiate resources

You need to agree with your boss and your direct reports what will constitute success. When dealing with all of them, avoid surprises, recognise past successes and failings, be open and accessible and balance problems with opportunities. Also, recognise that, while people may change and develop their outlook, you'll need to work with people as they are now.

With your new boss, you also need to take responsibility for making the relationship work, clarifying expectations early and often. You should also negotiate timeframes for action – what will be achieved when – and find early successes that are important. Another priority is to secure the resources you need. This can be achieved by:

- **understanding the underlying interests of your boss and others whose support may be needed. How will they benefit by giving you the resources you want?;**
- **trying to find mutually beneficial solutions that both support your boss's agenda and your own. Similarly, look for ways to support your peers in return for their help;**
- **linking resources to results. Emphasise the benefits that more resources will bring and consider producing a menu of what can**

be achieved with current resources and what different-sized incremental increases will enable you to do.

Build your team

This is quite possibly the most important challenge for new senior executives and one where many stumble. Without the right team working effectively, success will be severely limited. So, what are the potential problems and what do you need to do? Potential pitfalls include: keeping the existing team for too long; failing to refocus the existing team on your top priorities; overlooking the need for team restructuring to be kept in line with the overall aims of the business and failing to retain good people and trying to do too much yourself. These difficulties can be avoided by:

- **assessing your existing team. Consider what matters to you and the business, and rate each team-member against these criteria. If you're unsure, then test their judgement and see how they perform;**
- **restructuring your team. This may mean assigning people into specific categories: people who you want to keep in place, promote, retain and develop, move laterally, observe for a while (on probation), replace as a low priority and replace as a high priority;**
- **aligning goals, incentives and measures to motivate people and focus them on priorities. This may mean adjusting incentives, reporting systems and operating procedures, as well as encouraging teamworking and developing a shared vision;**
- **deciding how you want the team to work. Start by understanding how members of the team are used to working, with the intention of preserving the best of what worked well and changing what didn't. Next, focus on the issues or levers that will enable you to build your own team. This means understanding the role each individual plays in the team, the frequency and agenda for team meetings, the way decisions are made and the strengths and weaknesses of your predecessor's style.**

Communicate your vision and stay focused

A real test of how skilled leaders are is their ability to create and communicate an effective vision for their team or business. This is what sustains both leader and team during good times and bad. One of the reasons that leaders come to the fore is because people generally need to know where they're going, what their priorities are and how the future might look. You need to provide a vision that's realistic, powerful, easy to communicate and understand, appealing or desirable, focused and adaptive. The vision should routinely guide the way people work.

Manage yourself

When taking on a new role, you need to stay confident, focused and balanced, exercising sound judgement. To do this:

- prepare yourself (at least mentally) before taking on the new role;
- avoid the pitfalls – being too hasty or moving in all directions at once, becoming isolated or overly familiar, being tired, brittle or stressed, or being too biased and subjective;
- allow time for self-reflection. Examine what's concerning you and what's encouraging you. Assess what's gone well and what's gone poorly. Think about your next priorities;
- build support systems, people whose judgement you can rely on, and make sure that your personal life is stable and secure.

TEACH ME

How can you improve the coachees' understanding of an issue or particular behaviour? The answer is by asking them to teach you – it's a great way to explore people's attitudes and actions and helps them to improve their self-awareness.

THE IDEA

When to use it: When coachees are fixated on an issue, or lacking in confidence, or behaving in a way that they want to change.

Summary: 'Teach me' is a valuable way to explore how coachees approach or feel about an issue – you just ask them to teach you, the coach, about it. This helps them to find clarity and understanding about something that may be instinctive or deeply engrained.

DESCRIPTION

A simple technique is to ask coachees to teach you, the coach, about how they approach an issue or feel about something. It is an easy request, for example:

'I don't know how that feels/how to do that, teach me.'

The coachees then explain how they feel or what they do, and in the process provide a greater level of insight and detail about an issue. This can be valuable as a coaching technique at any time, but particularly during the phases of the GROW model when you're discussing a specific situation (reality) and the coachees' options.

'Teach me' is useful in several ways:

- **it helps ensure that the coach understands the coachee;**
- **it enhances the coachee's self-awareness;**
- **it provides a starting point from which to explore an issue;**
- **it can sometimes highlight a negative process that is being used and is restricting the coachee's success.**

TEAMWORKING (BELBIN'S TEAM TYPES)

Working in teams has developed into a normal aspect of the way organisations are structured and tasks undertaken, yet it's a difficult and complex aspect of leadership. Meredith Belbin has devised a hugely popular method of understanding the ways that people work together in teams, identifying nine types of preferred ways that team members do this.

THE IDEA

When to use it: Whenever you need to build a team or develop teamwork.

Summary: Meredith Belbin identified nine different roles people tend to take when working in teams (see Meredith R. Belbin, *Team Roles at Work*, published by Butterworth Heinemann, 1996). Understanding these roles can be invaluable when making decisions or solving problems.

DESCRIPTION
Understanding team roles (or types)

Belbin's team types identify preferred ways of working, meaning that some people may exhibit characteristics from a number of categories but one style tends to dominate the way they work in a team. Understanding and managing these individual styles effectively is seen as being important in developing and leading effective teams.

Team role	Contribution to the team	Acceptable weaknesses
Plant	Creative, imaginative, unorthodox. Solves difficult problems.	Ignores details and can be too pre-occupied to communicate well.
Resource investigator	Extrovert, enthusiastic, communicative. Explores opportunities and develops contacts – vital when researching and implementing decisions.	Overoptimistic. Can lose interest once initial enthusiasm has passed.

Team role	Contribution to the team	Acceptable weaknesses
Co-ordinator	Mature, confident and a good organiser. Clarifies goals, promotes decisions and delegates well.	Can be seen as manipulative and sometimes offloads work.
Shaper	Challenging and dynamic – thrives on the pressure of decision making and problem solving. Possesses the drive and courage to overcome obstacles.	Prone to provocation. May offend people's feelings.
Monitor evaluator	Sober, strategic and discerning. Views all options and displays sound, accurate judgement.	Lacks drive and the ability to inspire others.
Teamworker	Co-operative, perceptive and diplomatic. Listens, builds and averts friction.	Can be indecisive in crunch situations.
Implementer	Disciplined, reliable and efficient. Turns ideas into practical actions and results.	Can be inflexible or slow to respond to new possibilities.
Completer finisher	Conscientious, anxious and seeks out errors and omissions. Delivers on time.	Can worry unduly (unsettling) and be reluctant to delegate.
Specialist	Single-minded, self-starting and dedicated. Provides valuable knowledge and skills that may be in short supply.	Concentrates on technicalities and may only contribute on a narrow front.

Features of a good team leader

It's useful to understand the qualities of a good team leader. The best team leaders display the following behaviours (consider where you or your team leaders are strong and also where – and how – you could improve).

- **Gain the trust and commitment of team members, relating to people as individuals.**
- **Mobilise and involve people in the team – getting the best from each person and motivating them.**
- **Recognise and unlock people's potential by *empowering* and *enabling*.**
- **Encourage people to solve problems.**
- **Provide opportunities to team members.**
- **Provide support.**

- Encourage people to innovate, experiment and take the initiative by fostering a positive, blame-free environment.
- Coach, facilitate and guide their team, often acting as a sounding-board.
- Co-ordinate team efforts, both *within* the team and with others *outside* the team.
- Establish a reward system that satisfies the needs both of the team as well as individuals.
- Promote on the basis of merit.
- Encourage people who have the desire to excel and the ability to work constructively with others.
- Encourage questions and foster open discussion.
- Be proactive in relationships.
- Inspire teamwork and mutual support.
- Stimulate action and excitement.
- Lead by example.
- Develop and clearly communicate a powerful vision, setting direction for the team.
- Show sensitivity, awareness and understanding, monitoring conflict and intervening before it becomes too destructive.
- Give and receive feedback.
- Set goals with team members and discuss expectations.
- Understand how teams work, and developa personal style for forming, developing and leading them.

Identifying and avoiding problems with teams

Problems that develop in teams are often highlighted by the following behaviours. Consider which are present in your team, why and how they can be avoided or resolved.

- People display characteristic or prolonged dissent against or unhappiness with the job, other team-members or the leader.
- People work independently.
- People change their working routine – for example increasing their out of hours working.

- Team members work at cross-purposes, undermining each other unintentionally or deliberately.
- Initiative and responsibility are lacking: people are told what to do or wait to be told what to do.
- People are cautious of each other, perhaps even afraid to clearly speak their mind, motives are not trusted and the atmosphere is overly political.
- Domineering members of the team restrict contributions from others.
- Tensions and conflicts increase and can become harder to resolve quickly and amicably.
- Team members don't participate in decisions affecting the team: they withdraw from the group and no longer feel personal responsibility for success or failure.

Features of a good team

As well as assessing your effectiveness or that of your team leader, it's also helpful to assess the team's overall effectiveness. What does the team do well, what could they improve and how?

- Individuals within the team recognise their mutual dependence on each other, and understand that this is the best way to achieve personal and team success (people don't waste time trying to achieve success at the expense of others).
- Team members work at understanding each other, and communicate honestly and openly.
- Team members take a mature view of conflict, realising that it's unavoidable, trying to resolve conflict as swiftly as possible, and looking to generate new ideas and understanding as a result.
- People feel a sense of pride and ownership in the team, and are committed to the team's success.
- Members trust, respect, encourage and support each other – sharing information and experience and communicating openly.

■ Individuals understand when the leader needs to act and make a decision (i.e. in an emergency or if there's a major problem or disagreement).

■ Team members are relaxed, determined and dynamic: they know the team and understand their own strengths and weaknesses.

The diagnostic questionnaire for Belbin's team role analysis can be accessed via Belbin Associates' website (www.belbin.com).

THINKING STRATEGICALLY

What is 'strategy'? An overused word, it's simply a plan for moving from where you are to where you want to be. Keeping this in mind requires a balance between 'big picture' thinking and a detailed approach – this is the ability to think strategically.

THE IDEA

When to use it: When coachees need to develop or implement a business strategy.

Summary: One issue that lies at the heart of business strategy and makes it particularly interesting is *choice*. Strategy in business has three essential elements: development, implementation and selling (meaning, obtaining commitment and buy-in). Underpinning all three is choice and the need to choose a distinctive position about:

- **who to target as customers (and who to avoid targeting);**
- **what products to offer;**
- **how to undertake related activities efficiently.**

DESCRIPTION

Strategy – what it is and why it matters

Strategy is all about making tough choices in three areas. It means deciding on the customers you'll target and, just as important, the customers you won't target. This requires a focus on customers, segmenting in ways that are most useful and productive. Strategic thinking also means choosing the products or services you'll offer and what product features or benefits to emphasise. Finally, it means choosing the activities you'll use to sell your selected product to your selected customer.

There are several significant points to note about successful strategies.

- They are flexible and adaptable, capable of responding to opportunities and unforeseen challenges.
- They guide the way people work and the decisions they make.
- They're an essential, constant guide to developing the business.
- They focus on customers as the surest route to profitable growth.
- They understand that the journey is as important as the destination, and both the means and the ends are important.

Strategies succeed by being as simple and compelling as possible, routinely guiding decisions. They're considered and relevant as well as aspirational; they're distinctive, sometimes even bold and audacious, and they play to a firm's strengths.

Developing your strategy

The task of business strategy is clear. It's to move the business from A to B by guiding people about how best to make this journey. This requires clarity and decisiveness: the ability to make choices and find a route to success that's distinctive and realistic.

Business strategy has three distinct phases:

1 analysis
2 planning
3 implementation

Analysis

Analysis leads to strong conclusions and decisions; it helps you to find the right direction. Analysis needs to be thorough, comprehensive and wide-ranging and to achieve this, one technique stands out: questioning.

The issues to analyse...	...and the questions to ask
Your market	What changes are affecting your customers and competitors? What are the trends and likely developments? What are customers' priorities and preferences? How will these affect your business?
Your business	What business are you in? How and why should the new plan differ from your previous approach? What would make your approach different, distinctive and competitive?
Profitability	Where does your business make money? Where do you lose money and how could you improve profitability? How accurate were previous forecasts and plans – what did the business learn from these experiences? Where are your competitors most profitable? What would it take to double your growth rate and profits?
Competitiveness	How competitive is your business? What are your strengths and how will you build on these? Where will growth come from: expansion or market share? Which competitors do you admire and why? Which competitors do your customers like and why?
Strengths and weaknesses	What skills, capabilities and resources underpin your success? How can you play to these strengths? How can you improve weaknesses? Which resources do you need to acquire and how?
Your customers	What do customers value and what are their needs and priorities? How are your customers changing? Are there new groups of customers you can target? How well do they know your products and brand? What do they think of you? How can you encourage them to stay longer, buy more, pay more or leave your competitors?
Innovation	How can your business become more innovative? What innovations do customers want? What would they value (even if they don't know it yet)? How will you make innovations pay? Can you prioritise potential innovations in terms of their ease, impact and return?

Planning

There are several stages in the strategy planning process and each one relies on the completed analysis.

- **Defining your purpose – this should summarise where you are now, where you want to be and how you'll change. If possible, this should be a definitive statement of future goals agreed with colleagues and stakeholders; it should be as brief and clear as possible, a statement of intent.**
- **Explaining your advantage – people will want to understand how the business will succeed and what success will look like.**

Therefore, you also need to prepare a brief statement explaining why customers will buy from you rather than anyone else. These competitive advantages must be clear and enduring.

- **Setting the boundaries** – it's important to be clear about the products and markets you'll deal in, and those you won't. Too many boundaries will make the strategy inflexible and cause frustration, too few boundaries and the team will be unable to focus clearly.
- **Prioritising** – the strategy needs to emphasise specific products, customers and markets that are the most profitable or significant. Employees should be given specific responsibilities, objectives and resources so that the potential of these priority areas can be realised. It can help to encourage debate about priorities so that people are focused and engaged, and to regularly review these priorities as circumstances change.
- **Budgeting** – the budget needs to meet the strategic objectives and help to provide financial control.

Implementation

- **Integrating the strategy** so it takes account of the realities of the business. It needs to be consistent with people's skills and the expectations of customers. The challenge is to avoid confusion or conflict.
- **Communicating** – the ability to communicate clearly is an essential aspect of developing and implementing a strategy. People need guidance, information, clarity, even reassurance. Several techniques can help to develop a leader's skills as a trusted communicator:
  - look out for body language;
  - ask questions – not only to improve your understanding but also to test assumptions;
  - summarise, giving an overview at the start of what you want to say, and finish by summarising what's been agreed;
  - maintain professionalism and control emotions, treating others as you'd wish to be treated;

- maintain trust and avoid rumours;
- react to ideas, not people;
- focus on the significance of the facts and evidence;
- avoid jumping to conclusions;
- listening for how things are said and what is not said.

- **Achieving short-term goals** as quick wins help to generate momentum.
- **Agreeing clear objectives** – these should be SMART (specific, measurable, achievable, relevant and time-constrained). People also need to be held personally accountable for achieving their objectives. This means setting milestones, agreeing limits of authority and discussing how best to proceed, as well as establishing a system to monitor and measure progress.

Other techniques for successful implementation can also be applied, depending on circumstances. These include:

- testing aspects of the strategy;
- coaching people so they've the required level of skills and confidence;
- ensuring that people are motivated, engaged and committed to the strategy;
- assessing and monitoring the risks with new initiatives;
- monitoring performance and reviewing operational targets.

TRANSACTIONAL ANALYSIS

Parent, adult or child? Transactional analysis (TA) brings greater self-awareness both to the coach and coachee.

THE IDEA

When to use it: Transactional analysis is relevant and useful at any stage of a coaching relationship. It is particularly valuable when seeking to understand someone's frame of mind – both as a coach or when helping a coachee to understand someone else.

Summary: The useful framework offered by psychiatrist Eric Berne's transactional analysis model asserts that:

- **every grown-up individual was once a child;**
- **everyone who survives into adult life has had functioning parents or someone in loco parentis to some degree;**
- **we can be taken over at some time by these different ego states. And they can exist side-by-side;**
- **we do not suddenly stop accessing and being affected by these states. The mind does not have a mechanism for a finite beginning and an end to the transitions from one to another. For instance, is there a period at which anyone says: 'On this day, I feel an adult'?**

Recognising and understanding these states can provide valuable, vital insights for coaches and coaches.

DESCRIPTION

Our interactions are affected by the frame of mind we are in at any given moment. A frame of mind produces behaviour that in turn will produce responses in others. Coaches often deal with issues caused by interpersonal interactions and the frame of mind at the time an issue developed. Transactional analysis uses the term 'ego states' to describe the three states of mind which produce certain behaviour and subsequent, responses. For instance, most people have at some time, been on the receiving end of a childish tantrum, be it from a junior colleague, a peer or someone in a senior position. So too have we behaved childishly and sometimes realised, sometimes not, that the behaviour was inappropriate. At other times, we may have caught ourselves sounding like our parents as we dish out our views on how things should be.

Sometimes people can be plunged into a childish response by the sound of another person's voice or by the way something is said, which may be the last thing the speaker was trying to do.

In summary, the three states are:

1 **parent – authoritarian, in charge, loving, wise, critical, severe, nurturing, approving, disapproving, judgemental;**
2 **adult – equal, rational, analytical, logical, non-emotional, respectful, objective;**
3 **child – childish, creative, playful, irresponsible.**

There are many possible consequences – both intended and unintended – that occur as a result of people accessing different ego-states within the coaching relationship.

So, how do we view ourselves in the coaching relationship?

The questions below are designed to help you access the right state of mind when coaching others, so that they can respond to you as an equal who is there to coach them.

- **What is your 'elevator pitch' that describes in 30 seconds what it is you do?**
- **What is the definition of coaching that your training has taught you?**
- **What will you do if the client asks you to be authoritarian or parental in giving them advice?**

TRANSCENDING LIMITING BELIEFS

Many of us have beliefs that limit our success. When your coachees learn how to move beyond their limiting beliefs, it's a critical first step towards becoming successful.

THE IDEA

When to use it: To build confidence, improve skills, develop greater creativity or enhance the way you make decisions and meet challenges.

Summary: You can learn how to identify the beliefs that are limiting you and then replace them with positive ones that promote success. This exercise will help you to identify and overcome limiting beliefs.

DESCRIPTION

This activity can either take the form of a coaching conversation, or you can ask coachees simply to answer each question in turn.

- **Identify a belief that you want to change** – this might be something that you feel unable to do but that others can, or a belief that results from an experience or conversation earlier in life.
- **Understand and define how the belief limits you** – what is the belief and what is its impact?
- **Decide how you want to be, act or feel** – why do you want this? What are the obstacles to feeling this way? How can they be removed? Is there action you can take or conversations that would help? Understand how you want to behave, act or feel in the future, in specific circumstances, and *then behave this way*.
- Finally, **create a turnaround statement** that recognises and affirms this desire or that gives you permission to be, act or feel this new way. How will things be different? How will you act without this limiting belief? And how, in practical terms, will things be better?

VISUALISATION AND FUTURE ORIENTATION

A person's ability to imagine a future enables them to take steps and actions that will help to create that future. Without knowing what you want and being able to conceptualise it will leave you meandering aimlessly without a direction or course of action.

Visualisation means enabling coachees to develop a coherent description of how their plans will develop in the future. A clear, dynamic vision provides a clear focus for action, guiding people's decisions at all levels and helping to instil confidence and resolve.

THE IDEA

When to use it: When guidance is needed or when people would benefit from a clear sense of direction.

Summary: An essential element of visualisation is future orientation – the ability to communicate a clear view of the future of a business: its aims and what it's achieving. Future orientation applies to managers at all levels, whereas visionary thinking is most relevant to senior and mid-level managers.

Visualisation techniques can equally well be used at a personal level, to enable someone to get a clear focus on a personal development or behavioural change goal.

It's often the case that, as managers, we tend to focus on managing for today but we're less effective at preparing for tomorrow. A defining role of leaders is their ability to set the right course and then take people with them.

DESCRIPTION
Why use visualisation?

A clear and dynamic vision of the future is valuable because it:

- inspires, mobilises and engages people, unlocking energy and commitment;
- provides a clear focus for the future, guiding actions and decisions at all levels;
- promotes confidence, determination and effectiveness.

Understanding the different types of vision within a business context

Visualisation can be usefully applied at several different levels:

Type of vision	Purpose and value	Characteristics
Overall vision for the organisation (corporate vision)	• Provides a clear direction and aspiration for the business. • Inspires, mobilises and engages people. • Guides behaviour and decisions at all levels (providing a starting point for other business visions).	Inspiring and aspirational, clearly setting the direction, tone and priorities for the whole organisation as well as informing customers and shareholders.
Vision for a business unit, department or team	• Provides a clear, guiding direction for the business unit, department or team. • Supports the overall vision by translating it into a realistic aspiration for the smaller team, sustaining commitment and energy.	Inspiring and directly relevant to the work of the team, it engages and mobilises people so they work together, contributing to the overall success of the business.
A vision of a specific task or outcome	• Provides a clear focus for action in a specific area or for a particular task. • Used when delegating, or when forming or re-forming a team.	Guides the way that the task or role is approached, ensuring a clear view of what success will look like.

(For further information see *Business Strategy* by Jeremy Kourdi, published by The Economist/Profile Books.)

Developing a compelling vision of the future

There's no single way to develop visionary thinking and future orientation; however, the following actions are designed to help you get started.

- **Decide what you want** – don't just accept what other people believe. Decide for yourself what will be important in the future.

- **Trust your intuition.** If you feel that a situation is changing and different, or if you've an idea that makes sense to you, explore it further.
- **Test your assumptions and tap into the future.** Insights don't readily come from old information, so look for trends and try to understand why things are changing, not just how.
- **Get people to understand and support the vision** by:
    - communicating in an exciting and practical way;
    - speaking positively so that people are intrigued, challenged and motivated;
    - being honest and open, trusting you and the vision;
    - bringing the vision to life, ideally with examples;
    - listening and acting on what people say;
    - encouraging people to see what the vision means for customers.
- **Remember the characteristics of progressive views of the future – they are:**
    - powerful. There are two elements here: the vision must be imaginable (i.e. you paint a clear picture of what it will look like); it must also excite and inspire as many people as possible;
    - communicable. It must be possible for the vision to be communicated to anyone quickly and easily;
    - desirable and realistic. The vision needs to appeal to customers, employees and stakeholders;
    - Focused. The vision needs to be specific and 'real-world' enough to guide decision-making;
    - Adaptive. The vision needs to be general enough to accommodate individual initiatives, and flexible enough to allow for changing conditions.

Avoiding problems

The vision needs to be flexible and able to cope with changing circumstances. If it's too rigid or inflexible, then it will be fatally flawed and doomed to failure. You might want to consider the following.

- **What are the weaknesses of this approach?**

- What are others doing, and how is the situation likely to alter over time?
- Are the people involved prepared (in terms of attitude) and skilled (in terms of ability) to react to changing situations? How can this be measured? What remedial action might be needed?
- What is likely to prevent you and your colleagues from fulfilling your vision?
- How will you and your colleagues pre-empt these challenges, or react to any unforeseen problems?

WELL-FORMED OUTCOMES

This technique combines confidence-building with planning and visualisation. The result for coachees is a powerful sense of drive, energy, commitment and self-belief.

THE IDEA

When to use it: When coachees lack belief in their ability to achieve a task.

Summary: This technique is based on several key principles. First, planning or visualising a *positive* outcome is motivating and more likely to succeed, because it means that individuals don't have to think about what they don't want or would rather avoid. A *negative* outcome may have force but not direction, so once you've avoided something there's no positive target to attain. Also, by writing down the results (or outcomes) they want to achieve, coachees are much more likely to succeed. It's worth remembering the adage that 'If you don't know where you're going, any road will do.'

DESCRIPTION

Action checklist for developing a well-formed outcome

Detailed below is a practical, action checklist to help coachees develop well-formed outcomes.

1 **Decide your outcome and write it down.**
2 **Test your outcome.**
   - Is it positive? (For example, 'I want to enjoy peak health' rather than 'I want to give up smoking'.)
   - Are you moving towards or away from it?
   - Have you avoided any reference to negative things?
3 **Consider what resources or experience you already have to help you achieve your outcome. This may include life experience, skills, personal qualities or financial resources. It's important to focus on what can be controlled. For example, a**

sprinter can't be responsible for how well someone else runs in a race, so an outcome like 'I will train myself to be in peak condition for the 100m race in three months' time' is a better choice than 'I will win this race,' which involves other athletes who aren't under the sprinter's control.

- Can you find or initiate what you need for this outcome? Can you maintain it once you've achieved it?
- Is it in your power alone? If not, where do you have control and where does control or influence rest with others?

4   **Make sure that the outcome is specific and focused. Also, check that the language is unambiguous.**

- When does the outcome start and finish?
- In what contexts or situations, or with what people, do you want to achieve this outcome?

5   **Monitor and measure success. It's important to know when you've achieved your outcome.**

- What will success look like?
- What will you actually see, hear and feel that convinces you of success? (For some people, what they hear may include internal dialogue.)
- When will you systematically review this outcome?
- If it's a long-term outcome, how often will you revisit it?
- How would someone else know you've achieved it?

   This last point is especially important if you're self-critical. Self-critical people tend not to enjoy the satisfaction that should be theirs, preferring instead to focus on areas for improvement. It's important, therefore, to be clear about the evidence of success, so that you know when to stop, celebrate and set new outcomes.

6   **Make sure you're committed to the outcome. Do you want the outcome enough to work consistently for it? If not, what would it take for you to be sufficiently motivated?**

7   **Use the best of the present situation. Don't ignore the past or your current situation; instead, consider:**

- What are the benefits of the present state?

- How can you incorporate the advantages of the present into your outcome?

8 **Understand what may change if you achieve your outcome. For example:**
   - What might you have to give up to achieve your goal?
   - What will be the full implications for you personally of achieving your outcome?
   - Who else might be impacted by changes linked to your outcome and what is their attitude?

9 **Reconcile this outcome with your values and beliefs. It helps to establish at the beginning the balance between the different things that are important to us, avoiding self-sabotage. Consider:**
   - What larger outcome is this part of?
   - How does this fit into who you are and your major beliefs?

10 **Plan the outcome and reflect on the sequence of events. For example:**
   - Is this what you specifically want or a way of getting something else that's important to you? If the latter, are there other ways of getting it?
   - Do you need to set smaller, intermediate outcomes?
   - Is all the useful detail written down clearly?
   - Most importantly, what's the next step?
     It's worth remembering the Chinese proverb: The journey of a thousand miles starts with a single step.

11 **Finally, consider whether confidence is an issue by asking:**
   - What's your level of confidence in your ability to succeed at this outcome?
   - If it is not 100 per cent, what are you going to do to build your self-belief?

Remembering well-formed outcomes with the PEAS model

You may not always have the full checklist with you when you want to arrive at a well-formed outcome. This model will help you to remember key elements.

- **Positive** – specify, in positive terms, what you want to achieve.
- **Evidence** – specify how you will know you've attained your outcome or goal.
- **Appropriate** – check your planned outcome by asking:
  - Does it fit with major values?
  - What might be lost as a result?
  - How can you go for a 'win-win' outcome?
  - Where and when do you want to achieve it?
- **Self-maintained** – commitment, planning and progress are vital, so ask yourself:
  - Can you start and maintain it?
  - What other resources do you need?
  - Who else has influence and how much?
  - What's the plan?
  - What's the first step?

THE WHEEL OF LIFE

The wheel of life is a great way to build a sense of perspective and self-awareness – and it also enables coaches to better understand their clients.

THE IDEA

When to use it: When individuals need to understand the relative importance of different parts of their life.

Summary: The wheel of life shows important areas of our life and it helps us improve our understanding of what's going on in each of these areas. For example, it enables us to reflect on how we feel about them, the state of our mental and emotional health, our sense of identity and purpose, and our values, beliefs and priorities. Also, it highlights the balance of investment in (and satisfaction with) each of these areas.

DESCRIPTION

To use the wheel of life, draw a circle with 12 segments:

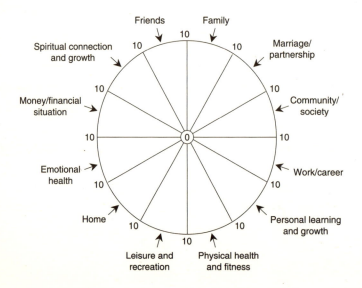

1 Reflect on each of the areas in turn and on what the words mean to you. Which areas do you typically invest most in? Why? What are the consequences? Rate each issue's importance to you on a scale from 1 (the lowest level) to 10 (the greatest level).

2 Which areas do you typically invest least in? Why? What are the consequences? Again, rate this on a scale from 1 (the lowest level) to 10 (the greatest level).

3 Which areas bring you the strongest sense of fulfilment, achievement and/or happiness? Why? What are the consequences?

4 Which areas bring you the strongest sense of uncertainty, dissatisfaction and/or failure? Why? What are the consequences?

5 Are there areas you find it particularly easy to reflect on in this way? Are there areas where such reflection seems particularly difficult or even pointless? What do these thoughts tell you about yourself?

6 Reflect on, for each area in turn, *your greatest achievements*. What are you proud of, in relation to that area of your life and why?

7 Reflect on, for each area in turn, *your current goals*. What do you most want to change/develop in relation to that area of your life, and why?

Finally, reflect on the implications of all your discoveries about yourself during this process and their implications for your goals. Where are there links between goals you have for yourself (and, if you're doing this yourself, your role as a coach to others)? How can you tap into the energy and sense of purpose such links can generate? Are there any conflicts between goals you have for yourself, and your role as a coach to others?

Be aware of how you personally approached this exercise, and what that tells you about yourself.

PART SIX

BIBLIOGRAPHY AND FURTHER READING

Area of interest	Suggested reading
Clarifying your concept of coaching	• Bandler, Richard and John Grinder. *The Structure of Magic*. Science & Behaviour Books, 1975. • Flaherty, James. *Coaching – Evoking Excellence in Others*. 3rd ed. Butterworth-Heinemann, 2010. • Leimon, Averil, Gladeana McMahon and Francois Moscovici. *Essential Business Coaching*. Routledge, 2005. • Rogers, Carl. *Client-Centred Therapy*. New ed. Constable, 2003. • Rosinski, Philippe. *Coaching Across Cultures*. Nicholas Brealey Publishing, 2003. • Peltier, Bruce. *The Psychology of Executive Coaching*. 2nd ed. Routledge, 2009. • Whitmore, John. *Coaching for Performance*. 4th ed. Nicholas Brealey Publishing, 2009. • Zeus, Perry and Suzanne Skiffington. *The Complete Guide to Coaching at Work*. McGraw-Hill, 2000.
MBTI	• Briggs Myers, Isabel. *Gifts Differing: Understanding Personality Type*. 2nd ed. Davies-Black Publishing, 1995. • Hirsh, Sandra Krebs and Jane A. G. Kise. *Introduction to Type and Coaching*. Consulting Psychologists Press, 2000.
FIRO-B	• Schutz, Will. *Firo B*. Consulting Psychologists Press, 1977. • Schutz, Will. *Firo: A Three-Dimensional Theory of Interpersonal Behaviour*. 3rd ed. Will Shutz Associates, 1998.
Rapport	• Maister, David, Charles Green and Robert Galford. *The Trusted Advisor*. New edition. Free Press, 2002. • Stone, Douglas, Bruce Patton and Sheila Heen. *Difficult Conversations*. Penguin, 2000. Patterson, Kerry, Joseph Grenny, Ron McMillan and Al Switzler. *Crucial Conversations: Tools for Talking When Stakes Are High*. 2nd ed. McGraw-Hill, 2011. • Thomas, Kenneth Wayne. *Thomas-Kilmann conflict mode instrument*, CPP Inc, 2002
General introduction to tools and techniques	• Bossons, Patricia, Sue Gover and Jane Cranwell-Ward. *Mentoring: A Henley Review of Best Practice*. Palgrave Macmillan, 2004. • Megginson, David and David Clutterbuck. *Techniques for Coaching and Mentoring*. Butterworth-Heinemann, 2004. • Zeus, Perry and Suzanne Skiffington. *The Coaching at Work Toolkit*. McGraw-Hill, 2002

Area of interest	Suggested reading
Specific approaches in greater depth	• Greene, Jane and Anthony M. Grant. *Solution-Focused Coaching*. Chartered Institute of Personnel and Development, 2006. • Lee, Graham. *Leadership Coaching*. Chartered Institute of Personnel and Development, 2003. • Levin, Michael. *On Bateson's logical levels of learning theory*. Massachusetts Institute of Technology, 1975. • O'Connell, Bill. *Solution-Focused Therapy*. 2nd ed. Sage Publications, 2005. • Pryor, Karen. *Don't Shoot the Dog*. 3rd ed. Ringpress Books, 2002.
Humanist approaches	• Bateson, Gregory. *Mind and Nature: A Necessary Unity (Advances in Systems Theory, Complexity & the Human Sciences)*. Hampton Press, 2002. • Kline, Nancy. *Time to Think*. Cassell Illustrated, 1998. • Kline, Nancy. *More Time to Think*. Fisher King Publishing, 2009. • Rogers, Carl. *Client-Centred Therapy*. New ed. Constable, 2003. • Pinker, Steven. *How The Mind Works*. New ed. Penguin, 2003. • Satir, Virginia. *People Making*. Science & Behaviour Books, 1994.
NLP-influenced approaches	• McLeod, Angus. *Performance Coaching: A Handbook for Managers, HR Professionals & Coaches*. Crown House Publishing, 2003. • McKenna, Paul. *Change Your Life in Seven Days*. Bantam Press, 2004. • Peltier, Bruce. *The Psychology of Executive Coaching*. 2nd ed. Routledge, 2009.
Other approaches	• Berne, Eric. *Transactional Analysis in Psychotherapy*. Souvenir Press, 1975. • Bradshaw, John. *The Family*. Health Communications, 1996. • Harris, Thomas Anthony. *I'm OK, You're OK*. New ed. Arrow Books, 1995. • Gerhardt, Sue. *Why Love Matters*. Routledge, 2004. • Lewis, Thomas, Fari Amini and Richard Lannon. *A General Theory of Love*. Vintage Books, 2001. • Passmore, Jonathan, et al. *Psychometrics in Coaching*. Kogan Page, 2008.
Coaching supervision	• Hawkins, Peter and Robin Shohet. *Supervision in the Helping Professions*. 3rd ed. Open University Press, 2007. • Hawkins, Peter and Nick Smith. *Coaching, Mentoring and Organisational Consultancy*. Open University Press, 2007.

Area of interest	Suggested reading
Solution-focused approaches	• Gallwey, W. Timothy. *The Inner Game of Tennis*. New ed. Pan Books, 1986. • George, Evan, Chris Iveson and Harvey Ratner. *Problem to Solution*. 2nd ed. BT Press, 1999. • Greene, Jane and Anthony M Grant. *Solution-focused Coaching*. Chartered Institute of Personnel and Development, 2006. • Jackson, Paul Z. and Mark McKergow. *The Solutions Focus*. 2nd ed. Nicholas Brealey, 2006. • O'Connell, Bill. *Solution-Focused Therapy*. 2nd ed. Sage Publications, 2005.
Leadership and teamwork	• Adair, John. *The Action-Centred Leader*. 2nd ed. Spiro Press, 1988. • Belbin, Meredith. *Team Roles at Work*. 2nd ed. Butterworth-Heinemann, 2010. • Charan, Ram, Stephen Drotter and James Noel. *The Leadership Pipeline*. Rev ed. Jossey-Bass, 2011. • Hawkins, Peter. *Leadership Team Coaching*. Kogan Page, 2011. • Kotter, John. *Leading Change*. Harvard Business School Press, 1996. • Kourdi, Jeremy and Sally Bibb. *A Question of Trust*. Cyan/Marshall Cavendish, 2007.
Strategy	• Collins, Jim. *Good to Great*. Random House, 2001. • Kaplan, Robert and David Norton. *The Balanced Scorecard*. Harvard Business School Press, 1996. • Sull, Donald. *Revival of the Fittest: Why Good Companies Go Bad and How Great Managers Remake Them*. Harvard Business School Press, 2003.
Personal effectiveness	• Al-Omari, Jehad. *Understanding the Arab Culture*. How To Books, 2008. • Blanchard, Ken, and Spencer Johnson. *The One Minute Manager*. Revised ed. HarperCollins, 2000. • Capodagli, Bill. *The Disney Way: Harnessing the Management Secrets of Disney in Your Company*. McGraw-Hill, 2001. • de Bono, Edward. *Six Thinking Hats*. New ed. Penguin, 2009. • Goleman, Daniel. *Emotional Intelligence*. Bloomsbury Publishing, 1996. • Hammond, John S., Ralph L. Keeney and Howard Raiffa. *Smart Choices: A Practical Guide to Making Better Decisions*. Harvard Business School Press, 1998. • Lewin, Kurt. *Resolving Social Conflicts and Field Theory in Social Science*. American Psychological Association, 1997. • Sartain, Denis and Maria Katsarou. *Under Pressure*. Marshall Cavendish, 2011.

INDEX